# CUSTOS

## TOTAL CONSECRATION THROUGH
# SAINT JOSEPH

THE 33-DAY PREPARATION FOR FULLNESS OF
DIVINE SONSHIP AND SPIRITUAL FATHERHOOD

DEVIN SCHADT

Excerpts from the English translation of the
*Catechism of the Catholic Church*, Second Edition,
©1994, 1997, 2000 by Libreria Editrice Vaticana,
United States Catholic Conference, Washington, D.C.
All rights reserved.

Unless otherwise noted,
Scripture quotations are from
the Douay-Rheims version of Sacred Scripture.
Copyright 1914 by John Murphy Company
Cover Design: Devin Schadt

© 2020 by Devin Schadt
All right reserved.

Stewardship: A Mission of Faith
11 BlackHawk Lane
Elizabethtown, PA 17022
StewardshipMission.org

ISBN: 978-1-7327739-6-7
Printed in the United States.

# Custos

## (Latin for Guardian)

*O St. Joseph, God Almighty granted you the heroic and noble duty of being Custos of the Blessed Virgin Mary, Custos of the Son of God, and Custos of the Holy Catholic Church. May I, by your powerful intercession, be as you are, a true and faithful guardian and protector of those for whom I am responsible.*

*St. Joseph, Custos of the Holy Family, Ora Pro Nobis*

# Contents

CUSTOS Quick Start ................................................. 7
CUSTOS Chart ...................................................... 8
Preparation for Consecration ...................................... 13

**STAGE 1: EMBRACE SILENCE | DAYS 1–6** ........................... 21
    Day 1: *The Silent Witness* ................................. 22
    Day 2: *The Secret King* .................................... 26
    Day 3: *The Mission's Origin* ............................... 30
    Day 4: *Just Like Joseph* ................................... 34
    Day 5: *The Custos* ......................................... 38
    Day 6: *The Path to Glory* .................................. 42

**STAGE 2: EMBRACE SECRET SACRIFICE | DAYS 7–12** ................. 47
    Day 7: *Listening* .......................................... 48
    Day 8: *The Call* ........................................... 52
    Day 9: *St. Joseph's Secret Weapon* ......................... 56
    Day 10: *Sacred Respect* .................................... 60
    Day 11: *Claiming Authority* ................................ 64
    Day 12: *The Obedient Man* .................................. 68

**STAGE 3: EMBRACE YOUR WIFE | DAYS 13–16** ....................... 73
    Day 13: *Embracing Woman* ................................... 74
    Day 14: *Submission to Authorities* ......................... 78
    Day 15: *Holy Detachment* ................................... 82
    Day 16: *The Contemplative* ................................. 86

+ JMJ +

**STAGE 4: EMBRACE THE CHILD | DAYS 17–21** .................... 91
    Day 17: *Inflicting the Wound* ................................. 92
    Day 18: *Claiming the Child* .................................... 96
    Day 19: *The Consecration* ..................................... 100
    Day 20: *Giving in Poverty* ..................................... 104
    Day 21: *Season of Preparation* ................................ 108

**STAGE 5: BUILD YOUR DOMESTIC CHURCH | DAYS 22–26** ............ 113
    Day 22: *A House of Worship* .................................. 114
    Day 23: *Sacrifice of Thanksgiving* ............................ 118
    Day 24: *The Enemy* ........................................... 122
    Day 25: *The Dark Night* ...................................... 126
    Day 26: *Guardian of the Soul* ................................ 130

**STAGE 6: LIVE THE LITURGICAL LIFE | DAYS 27–30** ................ 135
    Day 27: *A United Front* ...................................... 136
    Day 28: *The Ascent* .......................................... 140
    Day 29: *Losing Sight of Jesus* ................................ 144
    Day 30: *Seeking the Lost Child* ............................... 148

**STAGE 7: WORK FOR GOD | DAYS 31–33** ........................... 153
    Day 31: *The Father's Business* ................................ 154
    Day 32: *Holy Submission* ..................................... 158
    Day 33: *Surviving Spiritual Famine* ........................... 162

How to Make Your Consecration ................................. 167
Prayers ....................................................... 171
Custos Theological Reflections ................................ 179
The Thirty-Three Spiritual Practices .......................... 213
Notes ......................................................... 245

+ JMJ +

# CUSTOS Quick Start

**Step 1:** Review the suggested Spiritual Practices per each of the seven stages. See Spiritual Practices on p. 213.

**Step 2:** Select one or two of the suggested Spiritual Practices per each stage.

**Step 3:** Review the Spiritual Practices chart found on p. 8 and highlight or circle your selections.

**Step 4:** For those practices that are "To schedule" or are "1x To-Do's," plan ahead to determine how you will integrate them into your schedule.

**Step 5:** At the beginning of each stage of the consecration, review your practices and confirm your practice selections.

**Step 6:** Give yourself enough time in the morning and at night to fulfill your prayer promises.

**Step 7:** Be hopeful and persevere. Never give up. Do not let the devil convince you that you are a failure. Only the man who quits fails.

# CUSTOS QUICKSTART

## Step 1
Review the Seven Stages and their associated Spiritual Practices. (Descriptions begin on p. 213).

## Step 2
Select one or two of the suggested Spiritual Practices per each stage.

## Step 3
Review the Spiritual Practices chart (on the following pages) and mark your selections.

## Step 4
Plan ahead to determine how you will integrate the *1x To Do's* and *To Schedule* practices into your schedule.

## Step 5
At the beginning of each stage review the associated practices and confirm your practice selections.

## Step 6
Give yourself enough time in the morning and at night to fulfill your prayer promises.

## Step 7
Be hopeful and persevere. Never give up. Do not let the devil convince you that you are a failure. Only the man who quits, fails.

### STAGE 1
Embrace Silence
*Spiritual Practices 1-7*

### STAGE 2
Embrace Secret Sacrifice
*Spiritual Practices 8-11*

### STAGE 3
Embrace Your Wife
*Spiritual Practices 12-17*

### STAGE 4
Embrace Your Child
*Spiritual Practices 18-21*

### STAGE 5
Build Your Domestic Church
*Spiritual Practices 22-26*

### STAGE 6
Live the Liturgical Life
*Spiritual Practices 27-30*

### STAGE 7
Work for God
*Spiritual Practices 31-33*

# SAINT JOSEPH'S SEVEN STAGES | 33 SUGGESTED SPIRITUAL PRACTICES

1. Daily Morning Offering
2. Daily Litany of St. Joseph
3. Daily Examination of Conscience
4. Pray for Each Member of Your Family
5. Daily Morning Prayer (15 minutes / including 5 minutes of silence)
6. Daily Rosary
7. Evening Prayer (15 minutes / including 5 minutes of silence)
8. One Daily Hidden Significant Sacrifice
9. Reduce forms of media such as radio, music, news, videos
10. Avoid Grumbling About or Demeaning Family Members
11. Tithe Regularly / Give Charitably
12. Weekly / Biweekly Date with your Wife
13. One Daily Intentional Act of Encouragement / Affection to Your Wife
14. Be Faithful to Your Wedding Vows
15. Pray with Your Wife Once a Day
16. Bless Your Wife Daily
17. 10 Minutes of Daily Intentional Time with Your Wife
18. Biweekly Son Man-Date / Daughter-Date
19. One Daily Intentional Act of Encouragement or Affection to Your Child
20. Install Internet Filtration Software
21. Bless Your Child Daily
22. Family Dinner
23. Sacred Images
24. Sunday Gospel Reflection
25. Family Prayer Time
26. Family Evening Time
27. One Holy Hour a Week
28. Frequent Sacraments: Daily Mass with Child Once per Week / Monthly Confession
29. Establish Your Tent of Meeting
30. Celebrate Feast Days / Abide Fast Days
31. Abstain from All Work on Sunday
32. Initiate and be involved in Family Work
33. Sanctify Your Work

*Select one or two spiritual practices per each stage.
**Previous stage's spiritual practices are added to each next stage's practices

# CUSTOS
## TOTAL CONSECRATION THROUGH SAINT JOSEPH

## PRACTICES CHART

### PRAYER PROMISES

Morning Offering

Morning Prayer (15 minutes)

Litany to St. Joseph

Rosary / Consecration Prayer to Mary

Family Prayer Daily

Evening Prayer (15 minutes)

Pray with Wife Daily

Daily Examination of Conscience

Pray for Each Member of Your Family

### DAILY COMMITMENTS

Complete All Prayer Promises

One Hidden Sacrifice

Reduce Use of Radio / Noise and Listen to God

One Intentional Act of Encouragement / Affection to Wife

One Intentional Act of Encouragement / Affection to Children

Bless Your Wife and Children Daily

Give Your Wife 10 Minutes of Intentional Time (Focus on Her)

Family Dinner

Family Evening Time

### 1X TO DO'S

Establish Tent of Meeting

Sacred Images in Home

Install Internet Filtration

### PERSONAL PROMISES

Be Faithful to Wedding Vows / Be Pure

Abstain from All Work on Sunday

Initiate Serving / Work alongside Children

Avoid Grumbling and Complaining

### TO SCHEDULE

Date Night (Weekly / Biweekly)

Son Man-Date / Daughter-Date Biweekly

One Holy Hour Minimum Weekly

Take Child to Daily Mass Once a Week

Take Child to Confession Once a Month

Make Feast Days / Saints' Days Celebratory

Tithe Regularly

Family Gospel Reflection Weekly

# CUSTOS QUICKSTART

## Step 1
Review the Seven Stages and their associated Spiritual Practices. (Descriptions begin on p. 213).

## Step 2
Select one or two of the suggested Spiritual Practices per each stage.

## Step 3
Review the Spiritual Practices chart (to the left) and mark your selections.

## Step 4
Plan ahead to determine how you will integrate the *1x To Do's* and *To Schedule* practices into your schedule.

## Step 5
At the beginning of each stage review the associated practices and confirm your practice selections.

## Step 6
Give yourself enough time in the morning and at night to fulfill your prayer promises.

## Step 7
Be hopeful and persevere. Never give up. Do not let the devil convince you that you are a failure. Only the man who quits, fails.

+ JMJ +

# Preparation for Consecration

Why Another Consecration to St. Joseph?

We have Jesus, we have the Blessed Virgin Mary, and numerous saints who intercede on our behalf. Why do we need St. Joseph?

Jesus and Mary are the most compelling examples of faithfulness to God. Jesus was, and is, a son—the Son of God. Mary was, and is, a mother—the Mother of God the Son. Yet, as perfect as Jesus is, and as holy as Mary is, neither of them had the human vocation of fatherhood. Joseph alone was father and husband.

God appointed St. Joseph to be the husband of the Blessed Virgin Mary and to be a father to God the Son. God granted St. Joseph the incredible vocation of being the spiritual father, Custos (Latin for guardian) and leader of his holy family.

This is why St. Joseph is unique, and precisely why we need him. St. Joseph is the saint of husbands and fathers. His heroic fulfillment of his vocation shows us how to live our fatherly vocation. Not only does he show men how to live their vocation, but he relates to us personally. He understands the plights and perils that befall the family man who lives in a hostile world.

Yet, there is more. St. Joseph directs us to Jesus so that we may know Him intimately and be given the grace to become most trusting sons of God. This is very important. You and I cannot be dependable fathers if we do not first become sons who depend on

God the Father. St. Joseph directs us to Jesus, who teaches us how to become holy sons, and Jesus directs us to St. Joseph, who guides us to become holy fathers.

Our world tends to believe that there is no real difference between the roles and responsibilities of husbands and wives, or fathers and mothers. This consecration helps us to embrace and live that difference.

With that said, this consecration is not for everyone. This consecration is focused on St. Joseph's unique, essential fatherhood and headship of his family; therefore, it applies specifically to men, who are or will be fathers. By consecrating ourselves to St. Joseph, we fathers hope to become like him and follow his pattern of holiness.

Our Lord does not need us to be St. Joseph to Him. Nor does our Lady need us to be St. Joseph to her. No other person can be St. Joseph to Jesus and Mary. However, Jesus and Mary desire that we become faithful sons of God who then become mature men in Christ by being spiritual fathers. Yes, we are to become an image of St. Joseph to our family. Custos will help you to "go home and be Joseph" to your wife and children, friends, and coworkers.

## What's Unique About This Consecration

Why another consecration to St. Joseph? What is unique about this one? Though most consecrations focus exclusively on being consecrated to the Blessed Virgin Mary, or being consecrated to St. Joseph, this consecration is powerful because it follows the example of Jesus in a more true and complete way.

Consider that the God of the universe through whom, and for whom, all things were made, set aside His eternal glory, and

+ JMJ +

lowered Himself to be a little child, who was dependent upon Mary and Joseph for protection, provision, and love. With complete trust, Jesus radically and totally surrendered Himself to Mary and Joseph.

Jesus was not entrusted only to Mary. Nor was he entrusted to St. Joseph only. God entrusted Jesus to be Mary and Joseph's son. Mary did not consecrate Jesus to God alone. Joseph did not consecrate Jesus to God alone. Mary and Joseph were given the honorable responsibility to consecrate the infant Jesus to God—together. It was under these holy parents' care that Jesus prepared Himself for His mission to offer His life on behalf of us sinners.

So, what does this mean for you? To be a Christian is to follow Christ's example. To live your divine sonship fully, it is essential to do what Jesus did. Christ entrusted himself completely and unreservedly to Mary and Joseph. Following our Lord's example, we grant these spiritual parents our permission to shape us into an image of God the Son. Mary and Joseph by themselves cannot form us into images of God the Son, but because of their special relationship with Jesus and the Holy Spirit they obtain for us powerful graces that other saints cannot.

At the moment of His conception, Jesus became a member of the Holy Family. Similarly, after our baptism, the Holy Spirit dwelled in us, making us sons of God and members of a universal family known as the Church. The Church is comprised of saints in heaven, holy souls in purgatory, and those striving for heaven on earth. The Church's human members have Mary and Joseph for their spiritual parents.

But it is not enough to be born into a family. We need to grow up. Mary and Joseph continued to "raise" Jesus into mature manhood well after His consecration to God. Similarly, this consecration helps us live daily with Joseph and Mary and allow them to raise us to be faithful sons who become faithful fathers.

## What You Are Taking On

Usually goals that are important are difficult to achieve. If it is easy to be a gold medalist no one would consider it a great achievement. If it is easy to be a saint, we would not laud them as having accomplished a most tremendous ideal. This consecration is challenging because it has great potential to set us on the path to becoming a saint.

Custos is unique because it is comprised of daily meditations, prayers, *and spiritual practices*. The spiritual practices are specifically designed to help husbands and fathers experience personal transformation *and relational transformation*.

This consecration is not only about transforming you, but about the transformation of your relationship with God, the Blessed Mother, St. Joseph, your wife, and your children. This consecration is "total" not only because we totally surrender ourselves to Mary and Joseph, but also because it affects nearly every aspect of our lives.

Custos spans thirty-three days. Each day consists of a reflection based on those Scripture passages that recount St. Joseph's life. We only go as far as the Sacred Scripture allows. Therefore, we will not rely on private revelations regarding St. Joseph. This will help us follow St. Joseph as his life unfolds scripturally and reflect on who he is and how he relates to us.

The thirty-three days are segmented into seven stages. Each stage focuses on a certain principle of St. Joseph's life. To make

+ JMJ +

this consecration become a lived experience, each stage has several suggested Spiritual Practices. Prior to each stage, the participant selects one or two of the suggested Spiritual Practices associated with that stage. Each stage's practices build upon and are added to the practices of the previous stages. It is important to begin small, with one or two practices, and do them well.

Years ago, on Ash Wednesday, our parish priest encouraged us not to "give up" something temporarily during Lent. Instead he challenged us "take on" a spiritual practice during Lent and continue to do it for the remainder of our lives. I took his advice. Two decades later, many of my spiritual practices consist of those that I took on each Lent. This principle is life-changing. This is the idea behind the combination of reflections, prayers, and ongoing spiritual practices. During this consecration, we take on these spiritual practices with the goal of incorporating them into our life beyond the completion of the thirty-three days.

We do not want this consecration to be a one and done. So often programs inspire us temporarily, but the way we live changes very little. Custos is designed to help men experience ongoing transformation. Day 33 is not the end, but rather a new beginning. These thirty-three days are like a spiritual boot camp with St. Joseph. He will train you in his way of life, fatherhood, and holiness—if you humbly walk with him.

## The Effects of This Consecration

This consecration is life-changing because it helps us to conquer pride by becoming a little child. As Christ said, "Unless you become like a little child you will not enter the kingdom of Heaven." By going to St. Joseph daily you will gradually become dependent upon his spiritual fatherhood and will learn how to become dependent on Mary your Mother, and ultimately know how to worship Christ in spirit and truth. Consider yourself an apprentice in the strong and silent spiritual giant's workshop. He will train you to be a true spiritual father. But this depends on you first becoming his spiritual son.

Yet, we do not want only to be children. We must become mature men in Christ, spiritual fathers who are reflections of God our Father. By walking with St. Joseph for the next thirty-three days, you will learn from him how to be both a son and a father.

St. Joseph is the surest way to Mary. Mary and Joseph are the most certain way to Jesus. We are no longer orphans attempting to follow Jesus on our own. By radically surrendering ourselves to St. Joseph, he brings us to Mary, and the two of them give us special access to the heart of Jesus. We become an intimate member of the Holy Family. This is the surest and most secure form of consecration to Jesus because it was the way Christ was consecrated.

Thus, by totally surrendering ourselves to St. Joseph, he and Mary will consecrate us to Jesus, who alone is the Way, the Truth, and the Life.

The fruits of this consecration are a deep, abiding confidence and trust in God. No longer will you live in servile fear of God or be plagued by scrupulosity. Additionally, by being consecrated to St. Joseph, he will protect you from the devil as he protected Jesus from Herod. As a father you will be given the grace to fulfill the demands of the Gospel while living in this treacherous and sinful world.

You will become a child of St. Joseph and of the Blessed Virgin Mary. You will experience the fullness of divine sonship and become

+ JMJ +

capable of following Jesus your Lord more fully and intimately. You will become a father like St. Joseph, who is a human reflection of God the Father's benevolence, mercy, and relentless love.

After Day 33, if you stay the course you will experience a new beginning. Graces that were formerly veiled will become available by means of your humility and your intimate relationship with the Holy Spirit. You will have surrendered all that you are to Joseph, and he, for his part, will obtain all for you.

For a theological explanation of this consecration see p. 179, Custos Theological Reflections, including: Concerning the Act of Consecration; A Most Decisive Battle; Binding the Strong Man; St. Joseph Our Hope; The Purpose of This Consecration; True Imitation of Christ; Why Thirty-Three Days?; God's Intention and Plan; The Consecration Structure; Prayers and Practices and Motivations Matter.

For an overview of the suggested Spiritual Practices and their explanations see p. 213.

Stage 1

# Embrace Silence Days 1–6

During this first stage, we begin our consecration by learning from St. Joseph how to silence the worldly distractions that deaden our spiritual fervor and love for God. We embrace the silence and commit to fulfilling our prayer promises to better conform ourselves to receiving divine promptings, which summon us to embrace the lofty vocation of fatherhood more fully in Christ.

Suggested Spiritual Practices 1–7

# Day 1

INVOCATION: ST. JOSEPH, TEACH ME THE VALUE OF SILENCE

## The Silent Witness

*"Your Father Who is in secret." Mt 6:6*

Though the Gospels speak of St. Joseph, St. Joseph in the Gospels does not speak. What words can worthily describe a man whose words were not worthy of mentioning? Joseph's silence can often be misinterpreted as meaning he is unimportant, unnecessary, or a meaningless backdrop to the salvation story.

Joseph's silence, however, speaks profoundly of the effectiveness and essence of fatherhood. Joseph did not become a "voice crying out in the streets,"[i] or attempt to win the praise and honor of men.[ii] With simplicity, strength, and silence, Joseph resolutely persevered in becoming a father[iii] who saved the world by "raising"[iv] a Son who would become the world's savior.

✠ JMJ ✠

Joseph had no need to be popular, famous, noticed, an orator, or author, because his action—embracing Mary and raising Jesus—were ample testimony to his unwavering fidelity, enduring character, and fatherly strength. This type of silence speaks of the effectiveness of the spiritual father.

Joseph's fatherhood is a human reflection of the divine Father, "Who is in secret" (Mt 6:6). God the Father deliberately revealed His glory through His Word, His Son. Men of many words are often those who accomplish very little. The word of your secret fatherhood will one day be expressed in the child you have raised. This is the silent, strong, and effective essence of a father.

The hidden, unnoticed life of a father is a scandal to the world of pride and vanity. However, society goes by way of the family, and the family by way of the hidden father.

St. Joseph was a silent witness (Greek: martyr) whose enduring self-sacrifice has spoken profoundly of the glory of fatherhood. Your fatherhood does not need to sparkle, shine, or be proclaimed from the rooftops. You only need to be like St. Joseph, a silent martyr for your wife and children. This silent witness changes the world.

## Go to Joseph for Silent Confidence

At times we may be tempted to make our presence felt, or to be noticed and esteemed by others. The loud and proud appear strong, yet St. Joseph shows us that there is another way to live. Joseph was confident in God and therefore did not desire to make his presence felt. St. Joseph invites you to become like him and embrace the silent, sacrificial way of fatherhood. Today, your journey toward spiritual transformation has begun. How does silence relate to you? What ways do you struggle with silence? Go to Joseph and share with him those challenges, asking him to help you "silence the pride" that you may receive the inspirations of Christ.

—*St. Joseph, most silent and strong, please pray for me.*

## Concluding Prayer

*S*t. *Joseph, though you labored diligently, you were a man of intense prayer. You sought God in the silence. As a man, I am gravely tempted to busy myself with noble deeds, and to leave my mark on this world. As I embark upon this endeavor to consecrate myself to your care, please aid me in becoming like you, a man who embraces the silence, prays daily, and can discern the call of God most high.*

*O Most Holy Blessed Virgin Mary, St. Joseph her most chaste spouse, by your union of wills and your most holy intercession, please obtain for me that the Holy Spirit conceive in me ever anew, ever more fully, Jesus Christ.*

+ JMJ +

*Litany of St. Joseph p. 171*

FULFILL YOUR SELECTED SPIRITUAL PRACTICES FROM
STAGE 1: COMMIT TO EMBRACING SILENCE

*See Custos Spiritual Practices Chart on pp. 8–9*

# Day 2

INVOCATION: ST. JOSEPH, HELP ME TO EMBRACE MY WEAKNESSES

## THE SECRET KING
*"Do not be afraid . . . Joseph, Son of David." Mt 1:20*

St. Joseph was greeted by the angel of the Lord with the title "Joseph Son of David." This title is rich with significance for it connotes kingship. Joseph, whose blood was of royal stock, was the descendent of a long list of Jewish monarchs, and therefore heir to David's throne. Joseph was a king, yet a secret, hidden, unknown king.[v]

To be an heir to the throne of David, while living under the occupation of the Romans who hailed Caesar as not only king, but divine, would certainly make one an enemy of the Roman authorities. One who claimed to be king was a rival to Caesar, and therefore would be hunted and sentenced to death. It was imperative that Joseph's kingship remain hidden to ensure that eventually Christ the King would be revealed.

+ JMJ +

Joseph, Son of David, the hidden king, transmitted kingship to the King of Kings, the Son of David, Jesus, who when revealed as king was crucified for it.[vi]

Joseph's hidden kingship was revealed by the kingship of His Son. Though Joseph was a king because of David, his "father," he ultimately is king because of Christ the King, his Son.

Because of your baptism, and Christ living in you, you, like Joseph, are a secret, underground king.[vii] You are called to transfer the kingship, power, and dominion of God to your child. But as with Joseph, the ruler of this world, Satan,[viii] seeks to destroy the secret, father-king; for the father is a rival who has the power to overthrow the father of lies, by raising heirs of holiness.

Many men deny, neglect, or misuse their fatherly kingship. Many believe the lie that the secret, unknown, hidden father is useless, powerless, and ineffective. This is a demonic deception.

God calls you to be like St. Joseph; to receive, believe, and obey the angel's command, "Do not be afraid," you are a king in Christ who has Christ the King living within. Do not believe that your kingship and fatherhood is useless, powerless, and ineffective. Assume your kingly authority, embrace, and believe that God who lives in you[ix] grants you the power to become a godly father who, by your hidden kingship, will raise saints who reveal Christ to the world.

## Go to Joseph for Strength

Though we may often feel powerless over life, St. Joseph shows us that we are called to be like him: hidden kings of strength. But to be strong, we must first confess that we are weak. Where do you feel the weakest? In what areas of your life do you feel powerless? During this second day of your consecration, go to Joseph, your spiritual father, who understood what it felt like to be powerless. Expose to him your weakness and ask him to help you follow Jesus Christ, the King of Kings, more closely. Joseph is your spiritual mentor and guide and he will obtain the graces you need.

—*St. Joseph, a most hidden father-king,*
*help me follow Christ the King.*

## Concluding Prayer

St. Joseph, though at times you felt powerless over your life's circumstances, you consistently turned to God in your weakness. Though I want to appear as a man of strength, I too feel powerless and confess that I suffer from weakness. During this consecration, help me to trust that God's power and strength will be made known through my weakness. Help me to surrender myself to God in my hopes to be like Christ.

+ JMJ +

*O Most Holy Blessed Virgin Mary, St. Joseph her most chaste spouse, by your union of wills and your most holy intercession, please obtain for me that the Holy Spirit conceive in me ever anew, ever more fully, Jesus Christ.*

---

*Litany of St. Joseph p. 171*

---

FULFILL YOUR SELECTED SPIRITUAL PRACTICES FROM
STAGE 1: COMMIT TO EMBRACING SILENCE

*See Custos Spiritual Practices Chart on pp. 8–9*

# Day 3

INVOCATION: ST. JOSEPH, HELP ME BECOME DEPENDENT ON YOU

## THE MISSION'S ORIGIN

*"When Mary his mother had been betrothed to Joseph, but before they came together." Mt 1:18*

St. Joseph's espousal to Mary inaugurated his call to fatherly greatness. Enthralled by Mary's virginal purity, intense yet modest beauty, her unwavering holiness, her simplicity and singular devotion to God, Joseph was inspired to depart from the world of loneliness and isolation, and embark upon the mission of self-sacrificial and self-giving love by committing himself to living and dying for the Blessed Virgin Mary.

At the moment of Joseph's betrothal to Mary not only did his marriage begin,[x] but also an adventure that consisted of severe trials, intense hardships, and nearly insurmountable challenges.

+ JMJ +

From the moment that a man allows another person to occupy the dominion of his heart, it becomes vulnerable, and he risks being sorely tried and severely wounded.

The Sacrament of Marriage is an intense fire that purifies and perfects a man in his efforts to love his wife as Christ loves the Church.[xi] It purifies a man of his selfish tendencies and perfects him in self-giving love.

As St. Joseph allowed Mary into his heart, you have allowed your wife into your heart; and from that moment onward, you have entered the sacred mission of self-giving love. To grant your wife access to this sacred space indicates that you will be vulnerable to the painful process of purification. Along with this purification comes the temptation to flee from this holy mission. However, fulfillment is found in taking responsibility for woman and embracing her, rather than fleeing from her.

Every blessing has its curse and every curse has its blessing. For example, Jesus is the greatest blessing that Mary could ever receive. And yet, the blessing of His life ultimately ended in the curse of the bitter Passion of His death.[xii]

By means of your espousal to your wife you will receive some of the greatest blessings, but also endure bitter tests, trials, hardships, and purifications. Your commitment to this process is essential to your holiness—and your family's sanctification. Your glory as a father is intrinsically linked to your fidelity as a husband. To be an image of God the Father you must first be an image of Christ the Son, the Bridegroom who sacrifices Himself for His Bride. To truly succeed in this holy endeavor you will need to take Mary as your mother.

## Go to Joseph for Dependence

Though it may be difficult to see, you are beginning a life-changing journey with St. Joseph. He encountered tremendous challenges in his relationship with Mary. We all encounter difficulties in our marriages. What are the tensions and difficulties in your marriage? It is here, amidst these complexities, that St. Joseph comes alongside of you, calling you to shoulder up with him in carrying the cross. Depend on him. He understands your plight. Press on in your consecration to him. He will obtain for you the grace to persevere and become a true man of God.

—*St. Joseph, faithful husband, pray for me that
I may overcome the challenges of this day.*

## *Concluding Prayer*

St. Joseph, you experienced tremendous challenges in your calling to be the husband of Mary. Though my trials are not as severe as yours, nevertheless I often feel dismayed and even overwhelmed. During this consecration, I promise to depend on your spiritual guidance even more. Ask our Lord Jesus to grant me the strength that animated Him as He carried His Cross up Mount Calvary.

+ JMJ +

*O Most Holy Blessed Virgin Mary, St. Joseph her most chaste spouse, by your union of wills and your most holy intercession, please obtain for me that the Holy Spirit conceive in me ever anew, ever more fully, Jesus Christ.*

―――――

*Litany of St. Joseph p. 171*

―――――

FULFILL YOUR SELECTED SPIRITUAL PRACTICES FROM
STAGE 1: COMMIT TO EMBRACING SILENCE

*See Custos Spiritual Practices Chart on pp. 8–9*

# Day 4

INVOCATION: ST. JOSEPH, TEACH ME HOW TO TRUST

## JUST LIKE JOSEPH

*"But Joseph being a just man . . .
was minded to put her away privately." Mt 1:19*

Shortly after his betrothal (the first stage of Jewish marriage)[xiii] to Mary, St. Joseph was faced with a crushing crisis: his wife was pregnant without his cooperation.[xiv] According to the mandates of the Mosaic Law, a woman who became pregnant before the second stage of Jewish marriage (the solemnization) was to be executed by stoning as a consequence of her infidelity to her husband and to the Law.[xv]

The just man meditates on the law both day and night.[xvi] Therefore, St. Joseph, a "just man," knew the Law and its demands. Yet, he intentionally avoided the consequences of the virgin's apparent infraction and released Mary. If justice according to the Jew was measured by the Law and adherence to it, how could Joseph's dismissal of Mary and her perplexing pregnancy be understood as a just act?

To be just (Hebrew: *sadek*) is to be righteous as expressed by living in accordance with the Law, innocent of any charge, seeking God above all else. Could Joseph be such a man?

Joseph admired Mary's purity, holiness, and inner beauty, and therefore did not suspect that she had committed adultery.[xvii] He could not ignore the possibility that her pregnancy could be of divine origin. Yet, Joseph was also aware that he could not satisfy those who enforced the Law by proving Mary's innocence. Doing so would risk her being publicly shamed and executed. For Joseph this was an extremely confounding situation.

Joseph is just and innocent of charge because he did not dare to allow men to make a charge against Mary's innocence; rather Joseph waited upon God to shed light onto this dark dilemma.

In addition to this, Joseph is just because he did not cling to Mary, viewing her as the source and meaning of his life. St. Joseph was willing to release the creature in exchange for the Creator. The just man seeks God above all things and in all matters. Regardless of his intense love for Mary, Joseph refused to usurp the authority of God and presume that he was worthy of taking Mary and her child into his custody. Yet, St. Joseph remained open to God's holy will, allowing God to confer upon him the noble role of being a father to the Son of God. Because he surrendered Mary to God, God eventually surrendered Mary to Joseph.

You will be tempted on numerous occasions to make woman, your wife, sexual intercourse, and sexual desires the center and meaning of your life. You will be tempted to idolize the creature rather than worship the Creator. You will be tempted to violate God's law and the Church's teaching to ease hardship and tension in your marriage. As with St. Joseph, God has conferred upon you the noble role of being a husband and a father; and if you seek first God above all else, you will be just like Joseph and receive all things besides.[xviii]

### Go to Joseph for Trust

When things don't go the way we want, it is very tempting to become angry, frustrated or do something rash or foolish to regain control. But what if God wants you to grow rather than have control? St. Joseph experienced that temptation but overcame it by trusting in God. Are you having difficulty trusting God? Is there a situation that seems beyond His reach? Today, run to your spiritual father, St. Joseph and ask him to help you to be more open to God's will. He will show you how to let God claim authority over your life, and how to live the radical freedom that only Christ can give.

—*St. Joseph, most trustful, pray for me to allow God to have authority over my life.*

+ JMJ +

## Concluding Prayer

*St. Joseph, though you were gravely tested, you refrained from reacting rashly. You consistently turned to God with abandonment and unwavering trust. I am tempted often to retain control of my life and at times grow fearful of surrendering everything to God. As I persevere in my consecration, please obtain for me the ability to trust God completely and surrender myself entirely to Him.*

*O Most Holy Blessed Virgin Mary, St. Joseph her most chaste spouse, by your union of wills and your most holy intercession, please obtain for me that the Holy Spirit conceive in me ever anew, ever more fully, Jesus Christ.*

*Litany of St. Joseph p. 171*

FULFILL YOUR SELECTED SPIRITUAL PRACTICES FROM
STAGE 1: COMMIT TO EMBRACING SILENCE
*See Custos Spiritual Practices Chart on pp. 8–9*

# Day 5

INVOCATION: ST. JOSEPH, TEACH ME HOW TO PROTECT MY FAMILY

## THE CUSTOS

*But Joseph . . . was not willing publicly to expose her." Mt 1:19*

In the beginning, Adam was ordained with the mission to protect his sinless, virgin, wife, Eve.[xix] Yet, he failed.[xx] Where was Adam during that decisive moment of temptation, when the serpent pressed his doubts and allurements upon the soul of Eve? In the sacred text we discover an answer: "And she took of the fruit thereof, and did eat, and gave it to her husband who did eat."[xxi] Adam was there, present next to Eve, a silent witness and accomplice to evil. Adam allowed Eve to be exposed to the devil's cunning wiles.

At the beginning of the New Testament, a sinless, virgin woman did not take the "forbidden fruit" from a tree, in hopes to be "like

God,"[xxii] but rather she received God made flesh, the fruit of her womb, which eventually hung on a tree.

Joseph, a type of Adam,[xxiii] though uncertain of the origin of Mary's pregnancy, could have exposed her secret to the scrutiny, judgment, and condemnation of the Nazarene villagers and synagogue priests. Yet, Joseph does what the old Adam did not: he became the *Custos*, the guardian of woman. St. Joseph refused to expose Mary to judgment. Joseph refused to condemn his wife due to the possibility of her innocence. Within his spirit was a sliver of hope that a divine mystery was occurring in the Virgin's womb, and therefore he was unwilling to expose the possibility of such a sacred mystery to incredulous, doubting men.[xxiv]

You, my brother, as a husband, will experience the perennial temptation to expose your wife's shortfalls, failings, imperfections, intimacies, and internal mystery to others; to partake of her fruit and then expose her to the shame of men. You, however, are to be like St. Joseph, a *Custos*, guardian, protector of your wife's sacred mystery and God-given dignity. This is the mark of a New Adam: he upholds the dignity of woman by protecting her from the devil. Indeed, the evil one wants woman to expose herself for the purpose of obtaining disordered male gratification. You are to shield your wife from this temptation by loving her not for what she looks like or what she can give you—but for who she is.

## Go to Joseph for Perseverance

You have nearly completed the first stage of your consecration journey. You are not only working toward an end, but also toward an incredible new beginning. St. Joseph became the Custos, the guardian of Mary, and of Christ ... And of you. During this consecration, he wants you to clearly understand and know that he is your protector, your guardian, your guide, and your spiritual father. His intercession gives us new hope and trust in God. Even if you feel that you are not staying the course, return to St. Joseph and let him lead you.

—*St. Joseph, my guardian and guide, pray for me to persevere in this act of consecration.*

## Concluding Prayer

St. Joseph, you had the tremendous vocation of being the guardian of the Most Blessed Virgin Mary and the Son of God. You were entrusted with God's most precious treasures. I, too, have been entrusted with the gift of my wife and children. May this consecration teach me how to be a selfless protector of my family. St. Joseph be my protector.

+ JMJ +

*O Most Holy Blessed Virgin Mary, St. Joseph her most chaste spouse, by your union of wills and your most holy intercession, please obtain for me that the Holy Spirit conceive in me ever anew, ever more fully, Jesus Christ.*

---

*Litany of St. Joseph p. 171*

---

FULFILL YOUR SELECTED SPIRITUAL PRACTICES FROM
STAGE 1: COMMIT TO EMBRACING SILENCE

*See Custos Spiritual Practices Chart on pp. 8–9*

# Day 6

INVOCATION: ST. JOSEPH, TEACH ME THE MEANING OF GLORY

## THE PATH TO GLORY

*[Joseph] was minded to put [Mary] away privately." Mt 1:19*

A vocation is more than an occupation. Occupations are transient and changing and at the service of an exchange of goods. A vocation is a permanent covenant, at the service of an exchange of persons. An occupation can be defined as what you do for a living, whereas a vocation is defined by who you are living for.

The vocation of a husband and father is a divine call, a path to glory. Indeed, the Latin root word for vocation is *vox*, which means voice. It is in embracing and living his vocation that a man becomes capable of discerning the voice, the Word of God, that summons him to holiness.

+ JMJ +

St. Joseph was "minded to put [Mary] away privately." Some translations say that he considered divorcing Mary. This is an unworthy translation. The Greek word for "put her away" is *apoluó*, which means to "set free, release"; and while it can be used in the context of divorce, in this situation the word is qualified by the Greek word *lathra*, which means "secretly." To divorce Mary would indicate that Joseph would have subjected Mary to a legal procedure that would have exposed her to the judgments of men and the Law. Yet, to put her away privately indicates a positive, helpful action of hiding her away secretly, so as not to expose her to shame.

The virginal pregnancy instilled fear in the heart of Joseph, compelling him to separate himself from Mary, and thus inadvertently distance himself from his vocation of marriage and fatherhood. Joseph on one hand could have been afraid of the unknown origin of Mary's pregnancy and desired to void himself of any connection to, or responsibility for, the awkward and alarming situation. On the other hand, St. Joseph was overcome with a bewilderment, a holy fear, believing himself unworthy of the call to be the virgin husband and father of a child of supernatural origin.[xxv]

In either case, Joseph was tempted to separate himself from his vocational path.

You, my brother, will be intimidated by the devil, who by assailing you with various trials and tests will pressure you to withdraw from your vocation emotionally, spiritually, and physically. The evil one's goal is to convince you that you are not worthy of the vocation of fatherhood, or that it is not worthy of you. No one is truly worthy of this heroic calling; yet, this calling is worthy of every man. God, however, does not call the qualified as much as He qualifies the called.

Throughout the following reflections you will be granted insight into how you can overcome the devil's insidious doubts, your personal fear of failure, and "walk worthy of the vocation in which you are called . . ."[xxvi]

### Go to Joseph for Faith

You have successfully completed the first stage of your life-transforming journey with St. Joseph. This is cause for joy as you pursue your new way of life as a son of Joseph and Mary. But often after mountaintop experiences, the devil will instill doubts, fears, and allurements to push us from the path that we have embarked upon. When you experience the temptation to quit, or to neglect the spiritual practices that you have committed to, remember St. Joseph and his massive challenges. He understands how you feel. Ask him to help you begin anew and forge ahead in becoming a faithful child who will soon be consecrated fully in Christ to God the Father.

—*St. Joseph most faithful, pray for me.*

+ JMJ +

## Concluding Prayer

*St. Joseph, you became a saint by your vocation as a husband and father. This was your path to glorifying God and being glorified by God. At times, I am tempted to neglect this holy vocation, and even flee from its demands. As I complete this first stage of my consecration, please aid me with the grace you received to fulfill this divine calling with love and fidelity.*

*O Most Holy Blessed Virgin Mary, St. Joseph her most chaste spouse, by your union of wills and your most holy intercession, please obtain for me that the Holy Spirit conceive in me ever anew, ever more fully, Jesus Christ.*

---

*Litany of St. Joseph p. 171*

---

FULFILL YOUR SELECTED SPIRITUAL PRACTICES FROM
STAGE 1: COMMIT TO EMBRACING SILENCE

*See Custos Spiritual Practices Chart on pp. 8–9*

## Stage 2

# Embrace Secret Sacrifice Days 7–12

During this second stage, St. Joseph, the master of the interior life, teaches us the secret to making our prayers effective: hidden sacrifices. Therefore, by depriving ourselves of certain comforts, we strive to rid ourselves of those affections that slow the flesh and hinder the effectiveness of our fatherly intercession for our wife and children.

Suggested Spiritual Practices 8–11

# Day 7

INVOCATION: ST. JOSEPH, TEACH ME HOW TO LISTEN TO GOD

## LISTENING

*"But while he thought on these things, the angel of the Lord appeared to him in his sleep." Mt 1:20*

Why did Adam fail in the moment of temptation? He neglected to pray. St. John Vianney warns, "We don't find a sinner converted without turning to prayer. We will not find any sinner persevering without depending on prayer. Nor will we ever find a Christian who ends up damned whose downfall did not begin with a lack of prayer."

St. Joseph, a type of Adam, during his personal vocational crisis, "thought on these things [and] the angel of the Lord appeared to him in his sleep."[xxvii] Though Joseph was considering putting Mary away, he refused to act hastily, or come to a conclusion based on his presumptions. Rather, St. Joseph set himself apart, entered the silence, considered the matter, and ultimately submitted his dilemma to God.

Scoffers may contend that Joseph "had it easy" because angels appeared to him in dreams, offering certitude during his sore distress. Yet it is precisely because of his dedication to entering silence before God in prayer, and listening for God, that Joseph became capable of discerning the divine Word. Angels' voices do not enable a man to listen in prayer, but prayer enables a man to listen to the angels.

St. Joseph's determination to hear God's voice was so intense that his prayer continued deep into his sleep. The psalmist's words apply to St. Joseph: "I will bless the Lord who counsels me at night."[xxviii] Though a man may endure a spiritual dark night, if he but pray consistently, he will never lack God's guidance.

Trials, tests, tribulations, and crises will batter against and torment a man; yet the only man who is able to withstand such assailments without faltering is he who sets aside time to enter the silence with the intention of listening to God.

A man who withdraws from prayer will more likely withdraw from his vocation. A man who neglects prayer will be susceptible to neglecting his family. A man who protects his interior life is a man who protects his children and wife. The man who sets aside time, enters the silence, trains himself to listen for the *vox*, will certainly be guided by the divine compass.

## Go to Joseph for the Ability to Listen

Today we begin the second stage of our consecration: Embrace Secret Sacrifice. As men, we are doers and enjoy challenges.

But St. Joseph says, "Not so fast." He reminds us that a doer of the word must first hear the word. This demands that we listen for the Lord's promptings. Do you have trouble sitting still and waiting on God? If you do, you are not alone. Reflect on why you don't want to rest in God. Often, we avoid God because we don't want to face ourselves. What is it about yourself that you don't like? How would you like to be better? Ask St. Joseph for the courage to let God love you.

—*St. Joseph, master of the interior life, pray for me.*

## Concluding Prayer

*St. Joseph, you fulfilled the divine commands because you committed yourself to listening to God. I am often consumed by my work, my projects. I am often distracted and busy myself with the cares of life. As I begin this second stage of my consecration, I implore you to obtain for me the grace to rest silently in God, waiting upon Him without anxiousness, trusting that He will speak to my soul.*

+ JMJ +

*O Most Holy Blessed Virgin Mary, St. Joseph her most chaste spouse, by your union of wills and your most holy intercession, please obtain for me that the Holy Spirit conceive in me ever anew, ever more fully, Jesus Christ.*

---

*Litany of St. Joseph p. 171*

---

FULFILL YOUR SELECTED SPIRITUAL PRACTICES FROM
STAGE 2: COMMIT TO EMBRACE SECRET SACRIFICE

*See Custos Spiritual Practices Chart on pp. 8-9*

# Day 8

INVOCATION: ST. JOSEPH, TEACH ME THAT I AM NEEDED

## THE CALL
*"Joseph, son of David, fear not to take Mary thy wife." Mt 1:20*

By separating himself from Mary initially, unconsciously, and inadvertently, St. Joseph was separating himself from his vocational mission. Yet, God the Father relentlessly pursued Joseph, calling him to prayer. It was during prayer, in the midst of silence, while being attentive to God, that Joseph received confirmation of his calling and mission to be the husband of the Mother of God, and a father to God the Son.[xxix]

It is amidst silence, often in spiritual darkness, that you will discern the *vox*, the divine voice, which communicates and reveals God's vision, mission, and plan for your life. What is this mission? It is nothing less than to lead your family to communion and intimacy with God.

+ JMJ +

Though Mary is full of grace[xxx] and Jesus is full of grace and truth,[xxxi] without St. Joseph their family was not complete; they could not humanly, fully, express the Trinitarian glory of God, which is eternal self-giving love.[xxxii]

God is an eternal exchange of Persons; three divine Persons who are eternally and essentially One.[xxxiii] God created the family to be a living, breathing reflection, a human reminder of God's identity[xxxiv] (three Persons in one self-giving unity), and our destiny (union with the Trinity).[xxxv] God created the family as a human school wherein we learn to love like God.

Without St. Joseph, Mary and Jesus would not have become that human representation and reflection of the most holy Trinity.[xxxvi] Though Joseph is the least perfect member of the Holy Family, nevertheless God called him to set the pace of self-giving love, to ensure that his family would become that archetype, humanly speaking, of the Trinity and its self-giving love. In a certain sense, though without full knowledge of this mystery, Joseph was a guardian of the mystery of the Trinity in the family.

You also, must receive your mission to be a faithful husband and merciful father, who leads your family to relive, reveal, and reflect the love of the Trinity's eternal exchange of persons.

God "needed" St. Joseph to be a father to the Son of God because God the Son needed a human father. God the Father needs you to be a holy father, because your children need the Father of all holiness. Silence is essential.

By embracing silence and waiting upon God, He will reveal your mission and the means to accomplish this call to lead your family in self-giving love.

## GO TO JOSEPH FOR STEADFASTNESS

The pressure to perform, to provide, and to be strong for others weighs on us. Sometimes this pressure can become so intense that we want to run from our commitments. St. Joseph knows this feeling well. The situation with Mary's pregnancy instilled within the heart of Joseph a fear of not being needed, perhaps not being enough. What about you? Do you feel inadequate? Do you feel like you are unable to give your wife and children what they need? Go to Joseph. Share with him your concerns. Ask him to help you in these areas. He can obtain for you the most miraculous graces from his Son.

—*St. Joseph, most steadfast, pray for me.*

## *Concluding Prayer*

St. Joseph, though you were assailed by the temptation to feel as though you were unneeded when Mary was found pregnant with the Son of God, you trusted that God needed you. At times, I become overwhelmed by the pressure to be strong for others and, and I occasionally question whether I offer anything of value to

+ JMJ +

*anyone. May my consecration to you help me to trust that God needs me because my family needs God.*

*O Most Holy Blessed Virgin Mary, St. Joseph her most chaste spouse, by your union of wills and your most holy intercession, please obtain for me that the Holy Spirit conceive in me ever anew, ever more fully, Jesus Christ.*

*Litany of St. Joseph p. 171*

FULFILL YOUR SELECTED SPIRITUAL PRACTICES FROM
STAGE 2: COMMIT TO EMBRACE SECRET SACRIFICE

*See Custos Spiritual Practices Chart on pp. 8–9*

# Day 9

INVOCATION: ST. JOSEPH, TEACH ME TO LOVE THE BLESSED VIRGIN

## ST. JOSEPH'S SECRET WEAPON
*"That which is conceived in her is of the Holy Spirit."* Mt 1:20

God commanded Moses to make the Ark of the Lord from acacia wood and covered it in gold.[xxxvii] The ark was approximately two yards wide by three yards long[xxxviii] and was cherished as containing the very presence of God, for it contained the Ten Commandments;[xxxix] the manna from heaven in an urn;[xl] and Aaron's staff that budded an almond shoot.[xli] The glory cloud, the Holy Spirit, overshadowed (Greek, *episkiasei*) the Ark of the Lord.[xlii]

The Ark was Israel's secret weapon, which often was carried into battle, winning for the Jews decisive and often impossible victories. It was the Ark of the Lord that caused the walls of Jericho to crumble.[xliii] When the Israelites, led by Joshua, entered the promised land, it was the Ark, carried by the Levitical priests, that caused the waters of the Jordan to congeal at the city of Adam, enabling the Israelites to cross the riverbed dry shod.[xliv]

St. Luke, in his Gospel, draws a parallel association between the Ark of the Lord and Mary. The same Holy Spirit that overshadowed the Ark, overshadowed (*episkiasei*) Mary.[xlv] Mary contained the fulfillment of the ancient Ark's possessions: Jesus, the Word of God (the fulfillment of the Ten Commandments);[xlvi] the Bread of Life (the fulfillment of the manna from heaven);[xlvii] and the priesthood of Jesus (the fulfillment of the Levitical priesthood),[xlviii] the one who would rule the nations with an iron rod[xlix], the shoot of David (prefigured by Aaron's staff that budded an almond shoot).[l]

Indeed, as David proclaimed, "Who am I that the Ark of the Lord should come to me?"[li] When Mary greeted her pregnant cousin Elizabeth, Elizabeth exclaimed (cried out) "Who am I that the mother of my Lord should come to me?"[lii] The word Luke uses for "to cry out" (*anephonesen*) is an uncommon word, only used in Sacred Scripture in the context of a liturgical celebration wherein the Ark of the Lord was present. In other words, Luke is indicating that Mary is the fulfillment of the Ark of the Lord.

As the Ark of the Lord was the secret weapon of the Israelites, similarly Mary is the secret weapon of the Church and her faithful; for the presence of God is with her, and in her; as the angel of the Lord proclaims to her, "The Lord is with you."[liii]

The angel of the Lord commanded St. Joseph to "not fear" and to "take unto thee Mary," "for that which is conceived in her is of the Holy Spirit." When we withdraw from Mary, we withdraw from Jesus and the Holy Spirit. Yet, when we bring Mary into our hearts, she will obtain for us the power to topple the walls and crush the head of the adversary. She will restrain the waters of original sin, which flow from Adam, from drowning us in its effects. Indeed, if we like Joseph take Mary as our own, she will lead us safely to the promised land; for the Lord is with her.

### Go to Joseph for Devotion to Mary

A man can be tempted to believe that his wife holds him back. Or that he doesn't need her to become the man he desires to be. That was not the case for St. Joseph. He needed Mary. By taking Mary as his wife, Joseph received his vocation, his fatherhood; he grew in responsibility, exercised strength, and learned to love profoundly. Mary was the key to his success. She taught Joseph about love. Do you have trouble loving others? Do you have difficulty respecting your wife, her ideas, her counsel? Go to Joseph today. He will show you the secret to becoming a loving, heroic husband: devotion to and love for Mary.

—*St. Joseph, Guardian of the Blessed Virgin Mary, pray for me.*

+ JMJ +

## *Concluding Prayer*

*St. Joseph, by receiving Mary as your wife, you also received through her the grace to become a holy father and a faithful husband. As you depended upon and consecrated yourself to the Blessed Mother, please help me to surrender myself to her motherhood and forever be her son. May this consecration help me be a son in the image of the Son of God.*

*O Most Holy Blessed Virgin Mary, St. Joseph her most chaste spouse, by your union of wills and your most holy intercession, please obtain for me that the Holy Spirit conceive in me ever anew, ever more fully, Jesus Christ.*

*Litany of St. Joseph p. 171*

FULFILL YOUR SELECTED SPIRITUAL PRACTICES FROM
STAGE 2: COMMIT TO EMBRACE SECRET SACRIFICE
*See Custos Spiritual Practices Chart on pp. 8–9*

# Day 10

INVOCATION: ST. JOSEPH, TEACH ME TO BE DEPENDENT ON MARY

## SACRED RESPECT
*"Fear not to take Mary thy wife." Mt 1:20*

What instilled fear in the soul of St. Joseph? Some contend that his fear was induced by the angel's apparition. However, the angel's words disclose the source of his fear: he was "afraid to take Mary his wife."

Why would Joseph be fearful of committing himself to the Virgin who had committed herself to him? Joseph grew fearful because he was fully aware that Mary had consecrated herself to God, who had ordained that she be married to Joseph. Yet, the consecrated Virgin was now inexplicably pregnant. Mary's virginal consecration of herself to God appeared to run against the dominant beliefs and practices of the Jews, who birthed sons in hopes that one of them would be the greatly anticipated Messiah. Mary's vow of virginity, however, reflected more accurately the faith of the Jews who were familiar with the Scripture that a "Virgin would conceive and bear a son."[liv] Mary, who is the "Seat of Wisdom,"[lv] was aware of this prophecy, and therefore, as a fruit of her immaculate conception,[lvi] dedicated herself entirely to this hope. How can we know this?

When the angel of the Lord revealed that she would conceive and bear the Son of the Most High, Mary responded, "How can this be for I know not man?"[lvii] If Mary, who was betrothed to Joseph, had not made a vow of virginity she would have concluded that after the solemnization of her marriage to Joseph, the couple would unite in the one-flesh union, and the fruit of that union would be the Son of the Most High. Her words, "How can this be?" (meaning the conception of the Messiah in her), indicate that she had fully consecrated herself as a virgin to God.

Indeed, Mary "does not know man." She has not been tainted by the fallen tendencies and sinful disorders of man; for she had given herself completely to God.

Mary certainly disclosed to St. Joseph her vow of virginity. If this were not so, their marriage would be invalid and lack the true union of souls that constitutes an authentic marriage, for she would have intentionally withheld this vital information from her spouse.[lviii]

St. Joseph became fearful, for he being the just man who meditated on the law both day and night,[lix] was aware that "The virgin shall conceive and bear ... God with us";[lx] and the messiah shall shoot forth from David's line.[lxi] He was also aware that Uzzah inappropriately handled the Ark of the Lord, and because of this God smote him.[lxii] This instilled a holy fear in King David, who exclaimed, "Who am I that the Ark of the Lord should come to me?"[lxiii] Similar to David, Joseph, in the spirit of holy fear, believed, "Who am I that the Mother of my Lord should cometh to me"? St. Joseph became increasingly aware of the astounding holiness in Mary, which instilled within Joseph a holy fear, a sense of unworthiness before such an august mystery.[lxiv]

Joseph's fear of Mary was a holy fear, respect, awe, and reverence for the mystery she is, and the divine mystery she contained. It was Joseph's sacred respect for her that won from God the favor of being entrusted with God's greatest weapon: The New Ark, Mary.

Many men, Christian men, neglect or reject devotion and reverence to our Blessed Mother. How can the Lord accept a man who rejects His Mother? For by rejecting her, they reject Him, for the "Lord is with her."

If you desire to be respected as a father of glory, do as Joseph, the glorified father did: respect and be devoted to, and have a holy fear of the Mother of glory.

## GO TO JOSEPH FOR DEPENDENCE ON MARY

Independence, autonomy, self-reliance. Often these words are used to describe the rugged, self-made man. As men, we tend to believe that to depend on someone else is a sign of weakness, and to depend on a woman appears to be even weaker. St. Joseph could not have become the greatest husband and father on earth without Mary. To be consecrated to St. Joseph is to be consecrated to Mary. Together, as your parents in grace, they consecrate you totally to Jesus. Is there any aspect of Marian devotion that unsettles you?

*—Ask St. Joseph to show you how to love and respect the woman who helped to make him great . . . and she will do the same for you. Holy Mary, pray for me.*

+ JMJ +

## Concluding Prayer

*S*t. Joseph, I have noticed that many of the great saints entrusted themselves to Mary. Among them you were the first and perhaps the foremost. Though I am a grown man, I am humbled by the truth that I need a Mother. Please ask Mary to be my Mother, and to obtain for me the grace to be like the great saints who entrusted themselves to her.

*O Most Holy Blessed Virgin Mary, St. Joseph her most chaste spouse, by your union of wills and your most holy intercession, please obtain for me that the Holy Spirit conceive in me ever anew, ever more fully, Jesus Christ.*

*Litany of St. Joseph p. 171*

FULFILL YOUR SELECTED SPIRITUAL PRACTICES FROM
STAGE 2: COMMIT TO EMBRACE SECRET SACRIFICE

*See Custos Spiritual Practices Chart on pp. 8–9*

# Day 11

Invocation: St. Joseph, teach me how to surrender all to God

## Claiming Authority

*"Thou shalt call his name Jesus. For he shall save his people from their sins." Mt 1:21*

Upon receiving the angel's decree that disclosed the astounding news that the child in Mary was of the Holy Spirit, Joseph could have concluded that he was no longer necessary to Mary, and therefore been tempted to dismiss himself.[lxv]

Yet, the angel of the Lord confirms St. Joseph's essential, divinely ordained role by commanding him, "Thou shalt call His name Jesus." This command to give the child his name is no mere formality, or some type of token gesture given by God to affirm St. Joseph.

The act of giving a child his name, according to Jewish tradition and culture, was synonymous with claiming responsibility for, and authority over, the child. Considering this, the angel was expressing the fact that God had entrusted Jesus to Joseph's patronage and fatherly care. Indeed, by giving Joseph the command to give Jesus his name, the angel was declaring to Joseph that Jesus,[lxvi] the one who will "save his people from their sins," will soon enough need a savior to protect him (from Herod and for the people). Indeed, Joseph would become the savior of the Savior.

God, in a certain sense, needed St. Joseph to be a father, because God the Son needed a human father. God, in a certain sense, needed St. Joseph to be the spouse and servant-leader of Mary because Mary needed a spouse who would lead and lovingly donate himself to her.

Though this world falsely attempts to diminish and belittle the human father's role and authority, reducing him to being a placeholder or a token figurehead, stay the course. God needs you to be a holy father because your wife and children need the holiest Father, God. God needs fathers to lead, to save their families for the Savior. The human father is needed because the world needs the divine Father.

## Go to Joseph to Surrender

You have nearly completed the second stage of your consecration to St. Joseph. Perhaps you feel like you haven't fulfilled your spiritual practices perfectly. That's good. How can that be good? Because it shows that you can't do it yourself and therefore you need a savior. Though Joseph claimed Jesus as his child, St. Joseph ultimately claimed Jesus as his Savior. Do you find it difficult to claim your children for Christ? Sometimes that's difficult to do because we haven't allowed Christ to claim us. Ask St. Joseph to reveal those areas of your life where Jesus does not have authority. Then ask him to obtain the graces you need to surrender everything to Jesus,

—*St. Joseph's Savior, Lord Jesus, I surrender myself to you.*

## Concluding Prayer

*St. Joseph, though you claimed Jesus as your son, you also received Him as your savior. I too need a savior for I am a sinful man. During this consecration, I surrender all that I am to you that Jesus may have complete authority over my life. Claim me as your spiritual son that I may learn to be a true spiritual father.*

*O Most Holy Blessed Virgin Mary, St. Joseph her most chaste spouse, by your union of wills and your most holy intercession, please obtain for me that the Holy Spirit conceive in me ever anew, ever more fully, Jesus Christ.*

+ JMJ +

*Litany of St. Joseph p. 171*

Fulfill your selected spiritual practices from
Stage 2: Commit to Embrace Secret Sacrifice

*See Custos Spiritual Practices Chart on pp. 8–9*

# Day 12

INVOCATION: ST. JOSEPH, TEACH ME TO DESIRE TO BE OBEDIENT

## THE OBEDIENT MAN

*"So Joseph, arising from sleep, did as the angel of the Lord had commanded him." Mt 1:24*

Every father detests his child's disobedience. The human father's disdain for his child's disobedience reflects the heavenly Father's disappointment when His children disobey. "Because it is like the sin of witchcraft, to rebel and like the crime of idolatry to refuse to obey."[lxvii]

Consider that it was Adam's single act of disobedience that incurred the loss of paradise, the loss of impassibility (being incapable of suffering), immortality, and integrity; the rupture in his relationship with Eve and with God.[lxviii] It was this act of mistrust in the Father's love that conceived the sin inherited by each and every human being.[lxix]

+ JMJ +

After Adam awoke from his divinely induced slumber and received his wife, he eventually complied with her act of disobedience. By contrast, St. Joseph awoke from his sleep and did as the angel commanded him and took unto him his wife. As Adam's act of disobedience deterred the Trinity's love from being transmitted through the human family, Joseph's act of obedience is an essential component of his family becoming a human image of the Trinity's self-giving love.

The Latin word for obedience is *ob-audire*. *Ob* can be translated as "turning toward," while the word *audire* can be translated as "to hear."[lxx] In other words, an act of obedience always begins with the act of listening, particularly to God and His Word.

Humanity became subject to death because of Adam's fall. Yet, the human race begins to arise from mortality as Joseph arises in obedience to the angel's command. As with Adam and Joseph, your destiny, the destiny of your family and your descendants, is to a great extent dependent on your obedience, your ability to listen to God and respond appropriately. Obedience is the foundation of the life of every saint, and the foundation of your family in Christ.

## Go to Joseph for Obedience

You have completed the second stage of your spiritual journey with St. Joseph and are over one third of the way to your new beginning in Christ. By shouldering up with St. Joseph, he is teaching you how to carry the cross faithfully and obediently. Your prayer promises and spiritual practices are teaching you the essential characteristic of every saint:

obedience. St. Joseph "did" what he was commanded. Are there responsibilities in your life that you are resisting or putting off? Is there anything that you are not "doing" that you should be? Turn to Joseph, confess your disobedience, and ask him to help you love obedience. He will teach you that God desires obedience more than sacrifice.

—*St. Joseph most obedient, pray for me.*

## Concluding Prayer

*St. Joseph, Sacred Scripture attests that you were a righteous man and fulfilled God's commands. As I complete this second stage of my journey with you, I admit that there are moments wherein I am tempted to ignore the commands of God, or slow to do what I know is expected of me. Please obtain for me the grace to know what God is asking of me and to promptly fulfill His commands with humble obedience.*

*O Most Holy Blessed Virgin Mary, St. Joseph her most chaste spouse, by your union of wills and your most holy intercession, please obtain for me that the Holy Spirit conceive in me ever anew, ever more fully, Jesus Christ.*

+ JMJ +

*Litany of St. Joseph p. 171*

FULFILL YOUR SELECTED SPIRITUAL PRACTICES FROM
STAGE 2: COMMIT TO EMBRACE SECRET SACRIFICE

*See Custos Spiritual Practices Chart on pp. 8–9*

STAGE 3

# Embrace Your Wife
# Days 13–16

During this third stage our focus moves from personal transformation to the transformation of our marriage. We turn to St. Joseph, Guardian of the Blessed Virgin, and learn from his holy example how to overcome self-preoccupation, which chokes the growth of self-giving love. Therefore we strive to humbly serve our wives and bless them with our attention in hopes that they will receive more fully the love of the eternal Bridegroom Jesus Christ.

SUGGESTED SPIRITUAL PRACTICES 12–17

# Day 13

INVOCATION: ST. JOSEPH, TEACH ME HOW TO LOVE MY WIFE

## EMBRACING WOMAN

*"So Joseph, . . . took unto him his wife."* Mt 1:24

Consider, my brother, that the fall of mankind was determined by how the first man, Adam, failed to protect his bride.[lxxi] Consider also that the salvation of mankind was obtained by the eternal Bridegroom's sacrifice of himself for His bride.[lxxii]

A man's salvation, indeed, the level of his manhood, is determined by how he lives in relationship to woman, particularly his wife.

Etched in a man's body is his God-given mission: to be an initiator of self-giving love. Every man is determined by whether he strives to set the pace of self-donation continually and consistently in his attempt to achieve a deep, harmonious communion with his wife.[lxxiii]

+ JMJ +

A woman cannot forge a man into a man. However, God gives woman to man as the relational context in which God can make him into a saint.

In the Hebrew literature, a garden was often used as a symbol for woman and her fruitfulness.[lxxiv] The garden of Eden was the place where Adam failed to defend his wife, and the garden of Gethsemane was the place where Christ surrendered Himself as the ransom for his bride. Eden can be translated as meaning "delight," whereas Gethsemane means "oil press." By means of an association of terms, we can propose that the garden of woman can be a delight to man, but also a crucible that squeezes from him the "oil of charity."

St. Joseph's sanctity was forged and determined by how he lived in relationship to Mary. Mary was Joseph's delight, but also his Gethsemane. It was through Mary that Joseph learned to be pure, chaste, faithful, and sacrificial. Through Mary, Joseph received his fatherhood, his vocation, and his sainthood. Through Mary, Joseph received both trials and triumphs.

One of the keys to being an effective father is to be a husband who receives and embraces his wife's entire being.

It is through your wife that you have received your fatherhood, and eventually your sainthood. The threefold way to evaluate whether you are embracing the garden of woman and setting the pace of self-giving love for her is to ask yourself the following: First, do I bear my wife's burdens, faults, errors, idiosyncrasies as my own, as Christ bears the burdens of the Church as His own? Second, do I love my wife purely? Do I strive to overcome all temptations to lust for her, demean her, or lust after other women? Third, am I striving to donate myself to her authentically in hope of achieving an altruistic communion that reflects the union of Christ and His Church?

It is through your wife that you have received fatherhood and will achieve manhood, and by means of your self-donation to her, your sainthood.

### Go to Joseph for a Grace-Filled Marriage

Why can marriage be so difficult? Marriage is challenging because it is a most noble calling. The greater the mountain, the more difficult the climb. St. Joseph and Mary's marriage was the place where God the Son chose to dwell. Their marriage was the source of their family, and their family was a sign of God's Trinitarian love. And their marriage had challenges. Your marriage is the foundation of the Trinity's love being reflected in your family. As you enter this third stage of your consecration, reflect on those areas of your marriage that need healing. How could you love your wife better? Turn to Joseph and share with him your challenges. He will surely guide you.

—*St. Joseph, patron of all husbands, pray for me.*

+ JMJ +

## Concluding Prayer

*St. Joseph, your marriage was the foundation of your family, and your family was a living reflection of the Trinity's self-giving love. As I begin this third stage of my consecration journey, please obtain for me the grace needed to heal my marriage of any division, that my family can become like yours a living reflection of the Trinity.*

*O Most Holy Blessed Virgin Mary, St. Joseph her most chaste spouse, by your union of wills and your most holy intercession, please obtain for me that the Holy Spirit conceive in me ever anew, ever more fully, Jesus Christ.*

*Litany of St. Joseph p. 171*

FULFILL YOUR SELECTED SPIRITUAL PRACTICES FROM
STAGE 3: COMMIT TO EMBRACING YOUR WIFE

*See Custos Spiritual Practices Chart on pp. 8–9*

# Day 14

INVOCATION: ST. JOSEPH, TEACH ME HOW TO LEAD BY SERVING

## SUBMISSION TO AUTHORITIES

*"And Joseph ... went to Bethlehem ... to register, together with Mary his espoused wife, who was with child." Lk 2: 4-5*

Many people desire to be numbered among the saints, and yet neglect to be numbered among the people.[lxxv] Often a man idealizes sainthood as solely the demand to be intimate with God, while separating himself from people and their demands.

Yet, to love the Creator is to love his creatures, and God in His creatures; for "how can one love the God he cannot see if he loves not the people he does see?"[lxxvi] One cannot experience the exalted God, and being exalted by God, without the experience of being a humble servant of men, and being humbled by serving men.

+ JMJ +

A religious man can be more inclined to serve religious authority while neglecting to obey secular authorities. Yet, submission to a secular authority can often determine whether a man is truly religious.

St. Paul admonishes Christians, "Let everyone be subject to higher authorities, for there exist no other authority except from God, and those who exist have been appointed by God. Therefore, he who resists authority resists the ordinance of God; and they that resist bring on themselves condemnation."[lxxvii]

Often God uses secular authorities to determine if a servant be responsible in "small matters," and therefore be trusted with "greater responsibilities."[lxxviii] If a law does not compromise one's objective moral code, submission to the law must not be compromised.

St. Joseph humbly obeyed Caesar Augustus's dictate to be numbered among the peoples in the ruler's census. By submitting to a secular authority, Joseph enabled Jesus to be born and counted among the peoples[lxxix] whom He would save eventually, and to fulfill the prophecy that the Messiah be born in Bethlehem.[lxxx] By being obedient to worldly powers, Joseph allowed the power of God to be made manifest.

St. Joseph's submission to secular authority is a testimony of his trust in the God who gave men such authority. By submitting to an authority above himself, Joseph proves that he is worthy of his family's (Mary and Jesus) submission to his authority.

You, my brother, cannot lead others to obedience if you are unwilling to follow obediently. Obedience to employers, government leaders and especially religious superiors, is to be "numbered among the people," which enables a man to be numbered among the saints.

## Go to Joseph for Relational Transformation

Often spiritual programs are focused on personal transformation. While it is vital that we experience personal transformation, it is important that our personal transformation leads to relational transformation. That's one of the consequences of being consecrated to St. Joseph. Joseph shows us to depend on God for the grace to heal our relationships. St. Joseph teaches us how to serve. Serving brings healing. Do you have trouble serving your wife, your children? What are those things that you avoid doing that would show your family Christ's love? Ask St. Joseph to help you see the ways you can serve, and then act on it. By doing so, you and your relationships will experience transformation.

—*St. Joseph, servant of the Holy Family, pray for me.*

## *Concluding Prayer*

*St. Joseph, like Jesus, you chose not to be served but to serve. You did not allow the difficulties and challenges of life to convince you to feel sorry for yourself. I confess that there have been moments when the challenges of life weary me. It is during these occasions that the least thing I desire is to be at the service of*

+ JMJ +

*another. Lead me Joseph, to rise above my self-preoccupation and rejoice in serving my wife and children.*

*O Most Holy Blessed Virgin Mary, St. Joseph her most chaste spouse, by your union of wills and your most holy intercession, please obtain for me that the Holy Spirit conceive in me ever anew, ever more fully, Jesus Christ.*

―――――――

*Litany of St. Joseph p. 171*

―――――――

FULFILL YOUR SELECTED SPIRITUAL PRACTICES FROM
STAGE 3: COMMIT TO EMBRACING YOUR WIFE

*See Custos Spiritual Practices Chart on pp. 8–9*

# Day 15

INVOCATION: ST. JOSEPH, TEACH ME TRUE SELF-DETACHMENT

## HOLY DETACHMENT

*"And [Mary] brought forth her firstborn son . . . laid him in a manger, because there was no room for him in the inn."* Lk 2: 7

The true man is marked by his availability to God. He is the "free man" who does not allow self-will to prevent him from fulfilling the divine command. Such a man is a nuisance and danger to the devil and his plot to destroy God's Kingdom.

Most men, however, never experience such liberation. Too often a man is enslaved to his own will. He says, "Not my will, but Thine be done"; but lives "Not Thy will, but mine be done." He holds too tightly his personal ideas and believes that he knows with certainty the way things ought to be, and leaves little to chance. His days are marked by a pattern of personal protection with little vulnerability. He proclaims that God has control, while he attempts to control God; rather than God having his mind, he believes he has the mind of God.[lxxxi]

Often, men are enslaved to their own will, rather than being liberated by being slaves to the Holy Will of God. God's will come in many forms—some that are agreeable, others that are disagreeable, and yet all are profitable. St. Francis de Sales asks, "If I want only pure water, what does it matter to me whether it be brought in a vase of gold or of glass? What is it to me whether the will of God be presented to me in tribulation or consolation since I desire and seek only the Divine Will?"

When it was time for Mary, his wife, to give birth, Joseph was not able—even among his own kinsmen—to find suitable residence. Indeed, as with his Son, "His own received him not."[lxxxii] St. Joseph did not upbraid his Bethlehem kin for rejecting the Son of God, but rather detached himself from his own way of thinking and resolved to trust in God's providence.

Strength is found in trust, and trust is proven by detachment. Detachment from our own will, and acceptance of God's will, leads a man to new horizons upon which God can accomplish great good.

St. Joseph located a manger, and it was here that the Messiah was born in poverty. Joseph made himself available to God, casting aside his own personal ideas of how things ought to be, and because of this, God's prophetic plan of the Messiah being born in Bethlehem (meaning: town of bread) was fulfilled. The Bread of Life was born in the Town of Bread, and we, at every Holy Mass, have come to His humble trough to feed on Him—all because of Joseph's humble obedience.

Do you desire to be a man of greatness? Strive then to overcome the temptation to control God; and rather, allow Him control over you. Detach yourself from your narrow-mindedness and cease to think you have the mind of God. Attach yourself to the God who will broaden your mind to see His ways by means of blind trust, confirmed by holy detachment.

## Go to Joseph for Detachment

We all want security. We want the assurance that nothing will go wrong. Most of the time, things go as planned. But how do we react when things don't go our way? Often St. Joseph's "plans" were changed at the last minute. Life's circumstances, such as a census; or a miraculous, divine conception; or a manic, jealous, murderous king wanting to kill his son, put a wrench in his day. Joseph's secret to responding virtuously was detachment. Do you have situations in your life that make you angry, frustrated, overly worried? It could be that you are too attached to having things your way. St. Joseph wants to show you that by being detached, God can operate in your life and bring about great things.

—*St. Joseph, most detached, pray for me.*

+ JMJ +

## *Concluding Prayer*

*St. Joseph, time and time again, your life demonstrated that you were able to detach yourself from what you wanted. My personal bouts of anger, frustration, worry, and discouragement demonstrate to me that I am far too attached to my own desires. I beg you to teach me how to really believe, "Not my own will, but Thy will, O God, be done."*

> O Most Holy Blessed Virgin Mary, St. Joseph her most chaste spouse, by your union of wills and your most holy intercession, please obtain for me that the Holy Spirit conceive in me ever anew, ever more fully, Jesus Christ.

*Litany of St. Joseph p. 171*

FULFILL YOUR SELECTED SPIRITUAL PRACTICES FROM
STAGE 3: COMMIT TO EMBRACING YOUR WIFE

*See Custos Spiritual Practices Chart on pp. 8-9*

# Day 16

INVOCATION: ST. JOSEPH, TEACH ME HOW TO REST IN GOD

## The Contemplative

*"So [the shepherds] went with haste, and they found Mary and Joseph and the babe lying in the manger." Lk 2: 16*

Modern man, so disconnected from heavenly realities, often enslaves himself to worldly pursuits and ambitions, rarely perceiving the presence of Almighty God within him.

He lacks mastery over his own pathetic condition, for he lacks the strength that issues from the divine Master. He lacks divine power because he does not know the God of power who dwells within him. He fails to perceive the divine cry summoning him to a life of peace, because he resists being at peace. He fails to combat the worldly ruckus and clamor that bites at and bombards his ever-weary soul. He is driven to "seek the things that are below"[lxxxiii] incessantly. Such a man "lives according to the flesh and therefore minds the things of the flesh."[lxxxiv]

Yet, his world and these earthly trinkets will end abruptly, and if he does not become acquainted with, and reconnected to, that divine end, how tragic will his end be. How does the man addicted to progress, doing, and busyness, rise from his vicious mania and "seek the things that are above?"[lxxxv]

The shepherds witness a most serene scene: The Holy Family resting together in peace, huddled together, lying in the stable.[lxxxvi] The chill of poverty cannot penetrate the warmth and glow fueled by the furnace of familial love.

St. Joseph is a key witness to these sacred moments, but more so, an active participant in the mystery of divine, communal love in the human family. After searching for a suitable place for the Virgin to give birth, he surrenders his soul, mind, and body to contemplative rest. Joseph meditates upon the mysteries of the life of Jesus and Mary—the same mysteries that we identify as the Joyful Mysteries of the Most Holy Rosary—unfolding before him. Indeed, the saintly contemplative rests in the God-man who now rests with man. The guardian of the mystery of the Trinity pauses momentarily from his post as provider and protector and submits to tenderly and affectionately adoring the Madonna and Child.

A man will greatly benefit from systematically and intentionally resisting the constant busyness of modern life, its seemingly absolute demands to fix, accomplish, progress, compete, and complete; to resist idle entertainment and cozy-spirited, mind-numbing distractions; and rather rest in leisure by entering—with St. Joseph—into the mystery of the Trinity in the Holy Family.

By resting, personally, with the Holy Family in contemplation, you will be granted a desire to rest in leisure with your family. Cultivate the mystery of the Trinity in your family by means of holy conversation, familial prayer, and mutual affection. It is then that the mysteries of the Rosary become embodied in the human family, in your family.

### Go to Joseph for Contemplation

You have completed the third stage of your consecration to St. Joseph. If you keep the course, you will commit yourself to Joseph as a spiritual son; and he for his part, in union with Mary, will forever consecrate you to God. This consecration sets you apart as being sacred unto the Lord. The devil does not want this. He will encourage every type of distraction to keep you from completing your journey. St. Joseph had anxious concerns, much like you do. What causes the hurriedness, the anxiety in your life? What are the causes of your busyness? Share them with St. Joseph and ask him to show you how to rest in adoration of the Lord Jesus.

—*St. Joseph, true contemplative, pray for me.*

+ JMJ +

## Concluding Prayer

*St. Joseph, even amidst the most intense situations in which you provided for your family, you were able to find consolation in adoring the Christ Child. You teach me that being anxious about my problems does not solve them. You show me that stopping my hurried frenzy and taking a moment to adore my Lord Jesus, especially in the Most Blessed Sacrament, is the key to dealing with the difficulties of life.*

*O Most Holy Blessed Virgin Mary, St. Joseph her most chaste spouse,*
*by your union of wills and your most holy intercession, please obtain for me*
*that the Holy Spirit conceive in me ever anew, ever more fully, Jesus Christ.*

---

*Litany of St. Joseph p. 171*

---

FULFILL YOUR SELECTED SPIRITUAL PRACTICES FROM
STAGE 3: COMMIT TO EMBRACING YOUR WIFE

*See Custos Spiritual Practices Chart on pp. 8–9*

Stage 4

# Embrace the Child
# Days 17–21

During this fourth stage of our consecration we place ourselves under the guidance of St. Joseph, Guardian of the Son of God, to learn the art of claiming our children for God and raising them to be disciples of Christ. Therefore by acts of encouragement and time spent with our children, we endeavor to not merely accept our children, but rather choose our children that they may desire to choose God our Father.

Suggested Spiritual Practices 18–21

# Day 17

INVOCATION: ST. JOSEPH, TEACH ME HOW TO BE
PATIENT AMIDST TRIALS

## INFLICTING THE WOUND
*"And when eight days were fulfilled for his circumcision . . ." Lk 2: 21*

Discipline without love is abuse, and love without discipline is neglect. It is often said that if you do not discipline your child the world will. A father can discipline with mercy, but the discipline of the world is merciless.

Too often a father, fearful of his hidden strength and his inability to harness his passions, suppresses his duty to discipline believing that he is exercising virtue by granting his child liberation from laws. By being obedient to laws one discovers freedom; the neglect of laws enslaves a man in selfishness. A father who neglects to teach his child God's law is not virtuous but propagating vice.

+ JMJ +

Love can sometimes require wounding another. Indeed, often by wounding through discipline a person is healed of disobedience.[lxxxvii] St. Joseph, by circumcising Jesus, or having him circumcised, inflicted a wound that served as a perpetual reminder that being faithful to God will incur, inevitably, the shedding of blood.

A father is called to protect his child from suffering, while also training his child to suffer for God. Discipline is a regulated way to teach a child to suffer for what is true, good, and noble, while also helping a child to avoid useless suffering. Discipline causes a child short-term pain and long-term gain, whereas neglect of it grants short-term comfort and long-term pain.

The word "discipline" is derived from the Latin *disciplinus*, which means "pupil." The Greek word for "discipline" is *paideúō* which means "to instruct by training." The word "pedagogy" is also derived from this word. In other words, a father is a teacher, who forms his pupil, his child, often by discipline.

Indeed, the Greek word for "disciple" is *matethes*, which means "learner." A father trains his child in the ways of God through controlled, regulated, appropriate, discipline for the purpose of his child becoming the Lord's disciple, one who is capable of discerning and learning God's sovereign will. God's law, and obedience to it, serves as the means to train a child to be a disciple of Christ.

Yet if discipline is not regulated by love, the action becomes tyrannical abuse. Discipline must always be animated by love because the purpose of discipline is to teach a child how to love like God.

God the Father summons you to sainthood, perfection, and holiness. To be a son of the Father is to suffer, "for the Lord disciplines him whom He loves and chastises every son whom He receives."[lxxxviii] If you receive not God's discipline you will never be

God's disciple. If you neglect to discipline your child, your child will neglect God.

You will do well to imitate St. Joseph, who drew Jesus into God's covenant by means of discipline, which was associated with law. You are a teacher of God's law, whose noble duty it is to raise disciples unto the Lord by the appropriate use of discipline. Discipline your child while he is young, lest your child's rebellious decisions prove to discipline you.

### Go to Joseph for Patience

> When we encounter difficulties, we are tempted either to blame God for being against us, or to blame it on the devil, as though God were not involved. Often there is a middle ground: God is disciplining us. Punishment is for perfection and makes a boy into a man of God. By means of the many difficult circumstances that God permitted, St. Joseph experienced the Lord's discipline, and because of it he became perfected as a heroic, godly man. Do you feel as though God may be against you? Do you sometimes think God is absent? You are past the halfway mark of your consecration! Continue to rely on St. Joseph. Ask him to help you to trust that God is perfecting you into a holy man of God.

—*St. Joseph most patient, pray for me.*

+ JMJ +

## Concluding Prayer

St. Joseph, thank you for helping me complete over half of my consecration journey. Today I meditate upon your faithfulness in the face of great trials. I confess that on occasion I felt as though God had abandoned me, or simply wanted me to suffer. Please obtain for me the spiritual wisdom to understand and trust that these challenges are God's way of preparing me for perfection, for Himself.

*O Most Holy Blessed Virgin Mary, St. Joseph her most chaste spouse, by your union of wills and your most holy intercession, please obtain for me that the Holy Spirit conceive in me ever anew, ever more fully, Jesus Christ.*

*Litany of St. Joseph p. 171*

FULFILL YOUR SELECTED SPIRITUAL PRACTICES FROM
STAGE 4: COMMIT TO EMBRACE THE CHILD
*See Custos Spiritual Practices Chart on pp. 8–9*

# Day 18

INVOCATION: ST. JOSEPH, TEACH ME HOW TO LEAD MY FAMILY

## CLAIMING THE CHILD
*"And when eight days were fulfilled for his circumcision, his name was called Jesus, the name given Him by the angel before he was conceived in the womb."* Lk 2: 21
*"You (Joseph) will call his name Jesus."* Mt 1: 21

Having lost the understanding behind naming a child, often the modern parent selects for his or her children names that have little meaning or significance.

Peoples of ancient civilizations and various cultures were convinced that the act of a father naming his child was synonymous with claiming the child as his own, while also providing a prophetic clue regarding the child's identity, mission, and destiny, imparting a divine imprint upon the child's soul.

+ JMJ +

Consider the patriarch Jacob, the younger twin brother of Esau, who came forth during childbirth grasping his elder brother's ankle. He was named Jacob, which means "usurper." This name prophetically pointed to Jacob's destiny, in that he usurped his elder brother by stealing the blessing of the firstborn from his father, Isaac.

Moses, whose name means "drawn from water," as an infant was "drawn from water" by Pharaoh's daughter. Later, as a grown man, Moses led the Israelites dry shod through the Red Sea—through water—to their salvation.

Our Lord Jesus named Simon, his chief apostle, Peter, which is translated "rock." He likewise renamed Levi the tax collector Matthew, which is translated "gift of YHWH." By naming His apostles, Jesus was claiming them as His own, while also indicating their specific, unique identity and mission.

Responding to the divine command, "You shall call His name Jesus," St. Joseph did what all fathers are called to do: he called the child the name given by God, and by doing so, Joseph claimed Jesus as his own son.

In addition to this, the Jews traditionally named their child on the eighth day, when the child was circumcised. The circumcision of a son was the definitive statement that the father would raise his child in the religion of the Patriarchs.

By circumcising Jesus (or having him circumcised), Joseph did for Jesus what Jesus could not do for himself. Joseph helped Jesus fulfill the Mosaic Law and be counted among the Chosen People of God. Indeed Joseph, the father, enabled Jesus to enter and fulfill the Old Covenant, and because of this, Jesus the Son could enable Joseph to enter the New Covenant.

It is the noble honor of every father to seek the face of God, by means of prayer, and discern the name of his child, and to take this task seriously.

In addition to this, a father by means of the Sacrament of Baptism does for his child what the child cannot do for himself: he makes him a child of God by the Holy Spirit.

You also are called to lay the foundation of faith in Christ in your child by introducing him into the family of God, continuing to form the child; doing for your child what your child cannot do himself, in the hope that your child may one day do for himself what his father did.

### Go to Joseph for Confidence

Have you met someone who doesn't want to "impose" his religious beliefs on his child? He lets his child decide when he grows up. Can you imagine if we applied that type of logic to things like eating, studying, or working? "Don't impose that on him. Let him decide if he wants to work or eat when he grows up." St. Joseph understood that it was his duty to raise the child Jesus in the ways of Judaism. This was an incredible task. Do you feel unworthy to teach your children the ways of Christ? St. Joseph understands this feeling well. In what ways are you uncomfortable leading your family to God? Ask St. Joseph to help you become a spiritual leader in your home.

—*St. Joseph, head of the Holy Family, pray for me.*

+ JMJ +

## Concluding Prayer

St. Joseph, you had the incredibly intimidating task of raising the Son of God to mature manhood. Perhaps you felt unworthy of such a noble calling. I too sense my unworthiness and deficiencies in being the spiritual leader of my family. Help me to overcome any sense of personal insecurity or shame and obtain for me the courage to lead my family to God.

*O Most Holy Blessed Virgin Mary, St. Joseph her most chaste spouse, by your union of wills and your most holy intercession, please obtain for me that the Holy Spirit conceive in me ever anew, ever more fully, Jesus Christ.*

*Litany of St. Joseph p. 171*

FULFILL YOUR SELECTED SPIRITUAL PRACTICES FROM
STAGE 4: COMMIT TO EMBRACE THE CHILD
*See Custos Spiritual Practices Chart on pp. 8–9*

# Day 19

INVOCATION: ST. JOSEPH, TEACH ME HOW TO BE A CHILD OF GOD

## THE CONSECRATION

*"They took him up to Jerusalem to present Him to the Lord—
as it is written in the Law of the Lord, 'Every male
that opens the womb shall be called holy to the Lord.'" Lk 2: 24*

Mary and Joseph, after a new mother's forty days of purification, as mandated by Moses,[lxxxix] presented Jesus to God. This custom, known as the redemption of the firstborn, served as a reminder of the original Passover, when God spared the firstborn of all Israelites who were willing to consecrate themselves and their children to Him by the act of sacrifice, and of all the Egyptians who perished for their unwillingness to sacrifice to God.[xc]

This rite was accomplished by the parents returning their newborn child to God, and then, by purchasing the child back from

God with the price of a sacrifice, God would return the child to the parents.

This exchange is one of trust. The parents sacrificed unto God in order that the child might not be sacrificed to the devil. However, in this exchange, God entrusted His greatest gift of His Son to Mary and Joseph, who in turn entrusted Him to God; Who in turn delivered the child to them with the task of raising the child to fulfill His divine mission: to become the sacrificial Lamb of God.[xci]

Indeed, Mary and Joseph sacrificed unto God for the purpose of the child becoming a sacrifice unto God; they returned the child to God for the purpose that the holy child would give Himself completely to God.

A child can be likened to the talent in Jesus' parable.[xcii] A parent must invest in his child, and invest his child in the ways of God, that the child might return himself unto the Lord, bearing fruit unto eternity. Your child is on loan from God and must be returned and made capable of returning himself to God.

Children today are often viewed as inconveniences or encumbrances upon a parent's pursuit of comfort and freedom. Parents will do nearly anything—even murder—to avoid unwanted pregnancies. On the other hand, a child can be viewed wrongly as a temporal benefit to the parent, or a means to vicariously accomplish unfulfilled dreams. Yet, the child is a tremendous treasure in that he is the only thing (besides himself) a father can give to God that will endure for all eternity. A father's greatest joy is his child being born into eternal life.

By consecrating your child to God, you are sparing him from being sacrificed to the devil. A father cannot sacrifice his own child, but rather he entrusts his child to God in hopes that the child become a holy and pleasing sacrifice unto God. As with St. Joseph, God has entrusted you with the talent of your child, with the noble purpose of entrusting your child to God that the child may "be called holy to the Lord."[xciii]

### Go to Joseph to Be Consecrated

We are well over halfway through our consecration journey. Today's theme of consecration is very important. God wants you to be consecrated to Him. That is, set apart for something sacred, holy—something great. God has great plans for you, but it demands that you surrender and become like a little child. Just as Jesus surrendered himself to Mary and Joseph, and allowed them to consecrate Him to God, similarly you are to surrender yourself to these holy parents. They will do the rest. Be not afraid. You are in good company. The Son of God relied on Joseph to entrust Him to the Lord. We can do the same.

—*St. Joseph, my spiritual father, present me to God our Father.*

+ JMJ +

## Concluding Prayer

St. Joseph, you, and Mother Mary consecrated the Child Jesus to God. God allowed you to perform this sacred act of setting the Child Jesus apart for His holy mission. I too desire to be set apart, sacred, holy unto God. Please, in union with our Most Holy Mother, consecrate me to Jesus, that I may be totally consecrated to God.

*O Most Holy Blessed Virgin Mary, St. Joseph her most chaste spouse, by your union of wills and your most holy intercession, please obtain for me that the Holy Spirit conceive in me ever anew, ever more fully, Jesus Christ.*

*Litany of St. Joseph p. 171*

FULFILL YOUR SELECTED SPIRITUAL PRACTICES FROM
STAGE 4: COMMIT TO EMBRACE THE CHILD
*SSee Custos Spiritual Practices Chart on pp. 8–9*

# Day 20

INVOCATION: ST. JOSEPH, TEACH ME HOW TO BE THANKFUL

## GIVING IN POVERTY

*"And to offer a sacrifice according to what is said in the Law of the Lord, 'a pair of turtledoves or two young pigeons.'" Lk 2: 24*

There exist two types of men: graspers and givers. Most men toggle between these two poles. Tension in matters of money often exposes the interior man and his motivations: whether he is a man of mercy (generosity) or a man of mammon (greed and gain). Tithing, or making a return unto the Lord, heightens the ability to determine which of the two types he truly is.

Why does God, who is without need for money or sacrifices, require a man to tithe? Some men are wealthy, while others toil merely to scrape out a meager living. Whether a man be poor or rich, he is called by God to poverty of spirit,[xciv] a willingness to

+ JMJ +

humble himself and his money unto the Lord. Regardless of one's temporal poverty, a man is to give from that poverty to God.

Mary and Joseph's offering of two turtle doves was the "poor" man's offering in lieu of a lamb. St. Lawrence Justinian said that "grace raised the Virgin above the Law, but humility subjected her to it." The offering of Mary and Joseph was a sin offering made on behalf of the mother, which Mary, the sinless one,[xcv] had no need of offering. However, in humility Mary obeys. Similarly, St. Joseph, though temporally poor, exempts not himself, but instead humbly gives from his poverty.

To make a "return to the Lord for all that He has given"[xcvi] is to be humbly grateful, expressed by giving back to the Lord generously, without begrudging, "for God loves a cheerful giver."[xcvii]

Humility coupled with gratitude enables a man to make a return to the Lord despite his financial situation. Such poverty of spirit, as demonstrated by the widow's offering of the two copper coins (all that she possessed), is lauded by our Lord Jesus as the greatest offering.[xcviii]

A rich man is often afraid of giving from his wealth for fear that he will not have more; whereas a poor man is often fearful of giving from his poverty for fear that he will have even less.

The man who is "rich in spirit" measures his offering stingily, calculating his giving narrowly and precisely. Whereas the man who has poverty of spirit freely gives what God has prompted him to share. God will reward such a man: for God cannot—and will not—be outdone in generosity. Indeed, "he who sows sparingly will reap sparingly, and he who sows bountifully will reap bountifully."[xcix] Initially, Joseph may have been poor, but was eventually given the Magi's gold.

St. Joseph's poverty of spirit enabled him to give generously, even amidst temporal poverty, and because of this he was able to experience the joy of having the riches of Christ, whom he and Mary eventually gave to God. A man who is poor in spirit will not only share his money with God, but more important, his greatest "possession"—his child.

## Go to Joseph for Gratitude

Over the course of these days, St. Joseph is grooming you to be his spiritual son. Each day he reveals the secrets of a holy life. Today he wants to share with you one of the most profitable lessons: gratitude makes a man joyful. But to be thankful you will need to be poor. A poor person is thankful for everything, even the tiniest things. St. Joseph wants you to be thankful in all circumstances. This is to be poor in spirit; to not be so prideful as to demand more from God. Reflect on those areas where you may not be thankful.

—*St. Joseph, pray that I may be poor in spirit and rich in gratitude.*

+ JMJ +

## Concluding Prayer

*St. Joseph, as this fourth stage draws to a close, I thank you for taking me as your spiritual son. I sense that you are teaching me invaluable lessons regarding the spiritual life. Please help me to live them. I believe that you have chosen me and are training me as you trained Jesus. This inspires me to believe that God has chosen me as His own.*

*O Most Holy Blessed Virgin Mary, St. Joseph her most chaste spouse, by your union of wills and your most holy intercession, please obtain for me that the Holy Spirit conceive in me ever anew, ever more fully, Jesus Christ.*

---

*Litany of St. Joseph p. 171*

---

FULFILL YOUR SELECTED SPIRITUAL PRACTICES FROM
STAGE 4: COMMIT TO EMBRACE THE CHILD

*See Custos Spiritual Practices Chart on pp. 8–9*

# Day 21

INVOCATION: ST. JOSEPH, TEACH ME MAKE GOOD USE OF MY TIME

## SEASON OF PREPARATION

*"Behold, this child is destined for the fall and the rise of many in Israel, and for a sign that will be contradicted. And thy own soul a sword shall pierce that the thoughts of many hearts may be revealed." Lk 2: 34-35*

There are few duties as fundamental to a man as the protection of his wife and children. So sacrosanct is this mission that only a man with psychological difficulty can separate himself from this duty. The measure of a man can be determined by the level of sacrifice endured on behalf of his family. Our Lord confirms such a proposal: "Greater love than this no man hath, that a man lay down his life for his friends."ᶜ

Often a father fails to protect in the name of liberty, while others overprotect in the name of religion. Yet, if a wife and child

+ JMJ +

receive not the man's protection, they will seek refuge in false loves. If a wife and child are overprotected, they will rarely learn to defend themselves.

Upon hearing Simeon's foreboding prophecy that his Son would be contradicted and such persecution would pierce his wife's soul with sorrow, St. Joseph's heart was also pierced. The saintly guardian could not help but interpret such veiled language as indicating that he would not be present to protect and defend Mary and Jesus from this foreboding, ignominious fate. The words of Simeon were a sword that cut Joseph's heart.

A father's protection has boundaries not to be overstepped if his family is to grow in self-sacrifice. Although a man's protection has boundaries, his influence knows no bounds. A father is never to sacrifice his own child (by means of neglect or coercion), but rather spend his efforts helping to build his child into a temple of sacrifice. This is the supernatural goal of every father: to prepare the temple of his wife and child to become temples of self-sacrifice.

The season of preparation secretly slips by, often without warning. A man must keep vigil, arousing awareness, taking heed of the passing moments, transforming them into rites of passage.

Apply your efforts now, for soon you will no longer be able to protect and defend those you love. What you currently view as a burden, you will in hindsight count as a blessing. Today's duty that you desire to be relieved of, you will one day wish to relive.

St. Joseph could not be present at the time of Jesus' Visitation, lest perhaps he would have offered himself in place of his son. Joseph rather was hidden in the bosom of God the Father during Jesus' Crucifixion—with the Father, in a certain mystical sense, offering Jesus in sacrifice.

This is the sword of sorrow that pierces the heart of a loving, protecting father. After years of preparation, he must allow his child to go the path of self-sacrifice alone.

You and I, like St. Joseph, long after we have departed this mortal realm, may have great solace in the knowledge that we have participated with the Holy Spirit in helping our children become temples of sacrifice—if we seize the season of preparation.

### Go to Joseph to Appreciate Your Child

Often, we do not realize what we have until it's gone. Our children may pester us or cause us anguish. But when our life, or theirs, comes to an end, we will wish that we had loved them more. St. Joseph must have been pained by the knowledge that he would not be able to protect Jesus at His death. This caused Joseph to value each moment with Jesus as precious. As you conclude this fourth stage of our consecration ask yourself whether you struggle to appreciate your child. Go to Joseph and ask him to obtain for you the grace to make the most of your time with your child.

—*St. Joseph, exemplar of all fathers, pray for me.*

+ JMJ +

## Concluding Prayer

*St. Joseph, as I complete this fourth stage of my consecration, I reflect on the fragility of life. You sensed this fragility when Simeon foretold of Mary's sorrow and Christ's oblation. I spend much of my time preoccupied with worldly affairs. I often forget about God, and my wife and children's hearts, which hunger for Christ's love. Pray that I may seize this moment by pouring God's love into the hearts of my wife and children.*

*O Most Holy Blessed Virgin Mary, St. Joseph her most chaste spouse, by your union of wills and your most holy intercession, please obtain for me that the Holy Spirit conceive in me ever anew, ever more fully, Jesus Christ.*

*Litany of St. Joseph p. 171*

FULFILL YOUR SELECTED SPIRITUAL PRACTICES FROM
STAGE 4: COMMIT TO EMBRACE THE CHILD

*See Custos Spiritual Practices Chart on pp. 8–9*

Stage 5

# Build Your Domestic Church Days 22–26

During this fifth stage of our consecration we learn from St. Joseph, head of the Holy Family, the importance of becoming the priest of our family. By the use of sacred images, or reflecting on the Sunday's Gospel, or family prayer and family dinner, we attempt to establish a deeper connection between our domestic church and our heavenly home.

Suggested Spiritual Practices 22–26

# Day 22

INVOCATION: ST. JOSEPH, TEACH ME HOW TO
MAKE MY HOUSE A CHURCH FOR GOD

## A House of Worship

*"And entering the house [the Magi] found the child with his Mother Mary, and falling down they worshipped him."* Mt 2:11

It was between the event of the Christ Child's presentation and the unexpected visit of the Magi (approximately two years),[ci] that St. Joseph built or obtained a house in Bethlehem. Joseph was a *tekton*, a Greek word that means carpenter, architect, or builder. Joseph did indeed build a physical house, and yet it was this carpenter who, with God's aid, built the Holy Family into the first domestic church. In fact, it was within this house that the first gentiles fell down and worshipped Jesus as God. The Greek word for worship, *prosekynēsan* is translated as "to do homage, to adore, to prostrate oneself in reverence." Our Lord used this word regarding true worship of God the Father in His dialogue with the

Samaritan woman,[cii] and with the blind man whom He healed.[ciii] This indicates that the writers of the New Testament acclaimed, and worshipped Jesus as God.

In the event of the visit of the Magi, we come to the full realization that Joseph's house is indeed a house of worship. Such acts of homage elevated and inspired the heart of St. Joseph to a deeper, more reflective, contemplative worship (*prosekynēsan*) of Jesus.

The heavy responsibilities of fatherhood, perhaps even in St. Joseph's case, can often grind against and bear down on the man, making this heroic vocation appear common, mundane, lacking eternal significance, a ritual of life comprised of a series of ordinary events. Yet, like St. Joseph, a father is called to perceive the supernatural in the natural events, significance in the seemingly insignificant, the extraordinary in the apparently ordinary.

To overcome an overly pragmatic outlook on life, a father is to have a supernatural vision that allows him to perceive his temporal house as a domestic church, a place of worship.

In St. Joseph's case, his domestic environment was momentarily shaken by unexpected visitors. Yet, by hosting these visitors, Joseph witnessed his guests marvel over his child, thus rekindling awe and wonder within his heart.

St. Joseph saw the remarkable ability of the Magi to discern God in a human child. Every father is also called to perceive his child as a temple of God's presence, and even awaken his child to that reality by repeating the words of St. Paul: "Do you not know that you are a temple of God?"[civ] He should also keep in mind the words of our Lord Jesus: "Whoever receives a child in my name receives Me."[cv]

Your house is to become like St. Joseph's house: a house of prayer, worship, and communal gatherings in the name of Christ, which will afford your child experiences and memories that enable him to perceive himself as a temple of God.

Modern parents often mistakenly idolize their children, granting them greater adoration and attention than they give to God. A child must never be worshipped, even subconsciously, by the parent. A parent who approves of his child's immoral behavior has committed this sin.[cvi] Only God within the child is to be worshipped. Such respect for and awe of God's presence within your child will inevitably heighten the child's awareness of the reality that God lives within him.

You, the human father, have been appointed by God the Father to be a father who builds his family into a family like the Holy Family—into a domestic church wherein God abides. You cannot do this alone. When you intentionally unite yourself to God (who is in you), you allow God to establish your house as a house of worship, *prosekynēsan*; and by uniting yourself to God, your house of worship will be erected. Indeed, "Unless the Lord build the house, they labor in vain that build it."[cvii]

## Go to Joseph for True Authority

Today we reach a pivotal point in our consecration. We have journeyed with Joseph by embracing silence, hidden sacrifice, our wives, and our children. Today we begin embracing our charitable authority. God the Father wants his families to be led, and therefore raises up fathers to lead their families. St. Joseph was appointed by God to lead his family to God. To do this he established his house as a house of worship. The ultimate purpose of your leadership is to lead your family to God. Your house then should become a domestic church in which God dwells. What things are holding you back from making your home a domestic church?

+ JMJ +

—Ask St. Joseph to help you identify ways that you can make your family a "place" where God dwells.

## Concluding Prayer

*S*t. Joseph, your house was a house of worship. Some may think that it was easy for you to make your house a domestic church because God was your son. Surely it was a great challenge not to let the humanity of Christ eclipse your ability to worship His divinity. Please obtain for me the spiritual vision to see my family as more than a human institution, but rather, a holy domestic church for God.

*O Most Holy Blessed Virgin Mary, St. Joseph her most chaste spouse,*
*by your union of wills and your most holy intercession, please obtain for me*
*that the Holy Spirit conceive in me ever anew, ever more fully, Jesus Christ.*

*Litany of St. Joseph p. 171*

FULFILL YOUR SELECTED SPIRITUAL PRACTICES FROM
STAGE 5: COMMIT TO BUILDING YOUR DOMESTIC CHURCH
*See Custos Spiritual Practices Chart on pp. 8–9*

# Day 23

INVOCATION: ST. JOSEPH, TEACH ME HOW TO BE HUMBLE

## SACRIFICE OF THANKSGIVING

*"And opening their treasures they offered him gifts of gold, frankincense and myrrh." Mt 2: 11*

Right religion can be misunderstood as only abnegation, self-denial, a rigorous task of perpetual and precise self-renunciations. Although self-denial and the forgoing of certain favors is noble, admirable, and essential to the Christian who ascends toward sanctity, nevertheless one can fall prey to the temptation of denying the benevolence of God and his blessings. When a man submits to this error, he not only rejects God's blessings, but also rejects God Himself and His will. He believes that God's gifts are too great for him and rejects such favors in the name of false humility.

True humility recognizes that God is the giver of *all* good gifts.[cviii] The man who, admitting his own weakness, receives God's blessing and favor, rejoices and praises God with an ode of thanksgiving. This is precisely the response that God desires: "the sacrifice of thanksgiving."[cix] Thanksgiving in this manner is a sacrifice in that a man sacrifices his prideful refusal of any blessing he has not earned by his own powers, and rather acknowledges that all gifts are from God's providence and grace. He humbles himself before God by thanking him for all gifts received.

St. Joseph endured the harsh face of poverty in the form of a manger where the Mother of God gave birth to Jesus. Later, because of the Magi's gift, Joseph instantaneously became wealthy. St. Joseph did not reject the generosity of God given through the Magi, but rather received the gift. St. Joseph surrendered his will to the divine will of God, receiving the good and bad, poverty and wealth, in a spirit of true thanksgiving.

True self-renunciation is to renounce control of one's life, surrendering it to the divine will. God always rewards this type of renunciation.

The humble man's spirituality consists in acceptance of the good and bad, joys and suffering, riches, and poverty. He says with St. Paul, "I have learned, in whatever state, I am to be content. I know how to be brought low and I know how to abound."[cx] And therefore, Paul was "thankful in all circumstances."[cxi]

Rather than denying the gift of God, a man ought to humbly thank God for what he has received. Then, with a thankful heart, tithe a return of that gift as a sacrifice of thanksgiving. If you be rich, be "not proud or trust in the uncertainty of riches, but in God, who provides all things in abundance for our enjoyment . . . do good and be rich in good works, giving readily, sharing with others . . . in order that they may lay hold of true life."[cxii]

## Go to Joseph for Humility

We derive tremendous satisfaction from achieving a goal by our efforts and diligence. Often, we can misapply this dynamic to our spiritual life. While it is true that by fulfilling your prayer promises, spiritual practices, and daily reflections on St. Joseph, a personal relationship with him and our Lord is being formed. However, we must be careful not to believe that we are transforming ourselves. Only Christ can transform us. It was grace that transformed St. Joseph, and it is the grace of Christ that is transforming you. Jesus could not transform wine without water, and He will not transform your life without your efforts. Let us ask St. Joseph to help us to surrender, to do our best, and to let God do the transforming.

—*St. Joseph most humble, pray for me.*

## *Concluding Prayer*

*St. Joseph, you have taught me to embrace silence, commit myself to acts of secret sacrifice, to embrace my wife and children. Today, as I continue this fifth stage of our journey, I sense that God wants more from me. He desires that I be completely*

+ JMJ +

transformed. I cannot accomplish this on my own. Yet God won't do this without me. Obtain for me the courage to surrender all to you, to Mary, and to Jesus. I desire to be totally yours, for God and His Church.

*O Most Holy Blessed Virgin Mary, St. Joseph her most chaste spouse, by your union of wills and your most holy intercession, please obtain for me that the Holy Spirit conceive in me ever anew, ever more fully, Jesus Christ.*

*Litany of St. Joseph p. 171*

FULFILL YOUR SELECTED SPIRITUAL PRACTICES FROM
STAGE 5: COMMIT TO BUILDING YOUR DOMESTIC CHURCH

*See Custos Spiritual Practices Chart on pp. 8–9*

# Day 24

INVOCATION: ST. JOSEPH, TEACH ME TO TRUST IN YOUR PROTECTION

## THE ENEMY
*"Herod will seek to destroy Him." Mt 2:14*

Your child has an enemy whose goal is nothing less than the eternal destruction of his soul. It is this enemy, who is the father of lies,[cxiii] a murderer from the beginning,[cxiv] who comes to steal, kill, and destroy[cxv] your child's innocence and hope.

Childhood naivety and purity can often lure parents into believing that their children are far removed and buffered from the evils lurking and abounding in the adult realm. Yet, even before the child is born, the devil is poised to destroy him. "The dragon stood before the woman who was about to give birth, ready to devour the child as it was born."[cxvi]

Make no mistake, before a child sees the light of day, or draws his first breath, he is at war. It seems that the devil has an unfair

+ JMJ +

advantage—millennia of calculated deviant experience unleashed upon an innocent, uncomprehending being. Why is the evil one bent on destroying a child who appears to pose no serious threat to his diabolical kingdom? The child, by its mere existence, has the power to overcome the enemy. As the psalmist proclaims, "Out of the mouths of infants and of sucklings, Thou has perfected praise, because of thy enemies, that thou mayst destroy the enemy and the avenger."[cxvii]

Recall that God wills to relive, reflect, and reveal in our humanity who He is and what He does in eternity, God's identity is Trinitarian: three distinct, divine Persons who are one eternal union and essence, whose glory is infinite, self-giving love.[cxviii]

God intentionally created man and woman, who in their sexual distinction and difference compliment and complete each other. The ultimate fruit of their union is a child, an eternal soul; and it is this child who enables the couple to become a powerful living, breathing icon, a perpetual reminder of the Trinity. This reminder of the Trinity in the family is the "perfect praise" that "destroys the enemy and avenger."

The evil one will do anything to undermine and malign the sign of the Trinity in the family. His all-too-common tactics are marital divorce, infidelity, homosexual acts, pornography, the redefinition of the family and marriage, abortion, and contraception, and the like. He invents and utilizes ideologies such as modernism, hedonism, Marxism, communism, materialism and the like to assail the family for the purpose of deforming it into an anti-sign that is reminiscent of the isolation, bitterness, rupture, and shame of hell, rather than the glory of God's self-giving love.

Herod is a symbol of Satan who continually seeks to destroy the child, as He sought to destroy Christ. St. Joseph is a symbol of the human father who is commanded by God to shield and save the mother and her children.

You O human father are to be like St. Joseph, a guardian of the mystery of the Trinity in your family. The evil one despises this noble call and has identified you, your marriage, your family, and your child as a tremendous threat. Therefore, be on guard, "because your adversary the devil, is a roaring lion, goeth about seeking whom he may devour."[cxix] Resist him, strong in faith.[cxx]

### Go to Joseph for Protection

We know that we are to stand up for what is right. Yet, how many men surrender before engaging in battle? Often, to avoid the consequences of war we make deals with the enemy. The devil is your enemy. He convinces you that he will make things very difficult if you put up a fight. St. Joseph combated evil to save his wife and child.

St. Joseph understands what it is like to fall under the attack of the enemy. Ask yourself whether you have made deals with the devil to avoid raising your child for Christ. Today, turn to St. Joseph and ask him to be your protector and to help you protect.

—*St. Joseph guardian of Christ pray for me.*

+ JMJ +

## *Concluding Prayer*

St. Joseph, you are known as Terror of Demons. By overcoming the devil's intimidation, you most certainly are deserving of this title. I confess that I am not as strong. I sense that if I give myself totally to you, to God, that the devil will threaten and assail me. I need courage. Please help me to trust that by surrendering myself and my family to your protection, you will obtain every grace needed to persevere over sin and evil.

*O Most Holy Blessed Virgin Mary, St. Joseph her most chaste spouse,*
*by your union of wills and your most holy intercession, please obtain for me*
*that the Holy Spirit conceive in me ever anew, ever more fully, Jesus Christ.*

---

*Litany of St. Joseph p. 171*

---

FULFILL YOUR SELECTED SPIRITUAL PRACTICES FROM
STAGE 5: COMMIT TO BUILDING YOUR DOMESTIC CHURCH
*See Custos Spiritual Practices Chart on pp. 8–9*

# Day 25

INVOCATION: ST. JOSEPH, TEACH ME HOW TO EMBRACE HIDDENNESS

## THE DARK NIGHT

*"So [Joseph] arose and took the child and his mother by night and withdrew to Egypt." Mt 2: 14*

It was under the secret cloak of darkness that St. Joseph gathered his wife and the Child Jesus and escaped Herod's plot to murder the Christ. Herod is a symbol of the evil one who seeks to destroy the child. St. Joseph is a symbol of the human father who succeeds in shrouding and saving the mother, the child, and the family, by embracing the dark night of fatherhood in the foreign land of Egypt, a symbol of this world. This dark night consists of the humiliating and harsh reality of surrendering desire for fame, fortune, popularity, prestige, mammon, and gain in exchange for the daily investment in one's child, one's wife, one's family.

The father who embraces this night is often overcome by feelings of failure or inadequacy, sensing he has had no real or lasting impact, or influence on society; feeling as though his life is of little value; that he has not provided anything of true significance to the world. The obscurity of fatherhood and its apparent lackluster results can tempt a father to succumb to the temptation to believe that his child will find his own way, or that he must attend to greater matters, such as increasing his wealth or "finding himself."

The successful father does indeed flee from the world and its allurements (here we consider television programming, social media, movies, smartphone technology, all of which grant wide access to unrestricted, unfiltered, unregulated content). He intentionally chooses to reject those things that are in opposition to his child's purity; and subject the things of the world to his vocation for the purpose of raising saints who are not maligned by the Herods of the world.

All too many fathers view their child through the lens of their own personal lifetime of purification, holy perseverance, and redemption. Consider the vast amount of grace, personal effort, failings, and forgiveness you have endured and embraced only to achieve a minimal amount of freedom from sin and temptation.

Do not mistakenly believe that your child begins life at your sanctified level. The child is unfamiliar with the strategies of the evil one. Therefore, it is imperative that you aid him in identifying the enemy and instill in him the courage to flee from the devil.

Your example of fleeing from the enticements of the world is essential. A renewed awareness of and sensitivity to the devil's plots, strategies, and allurements aimed at robbing your child's innocence is necessary.

A father must have the heart of the heavenly Father, of whom Jesus said, "It is not my Father's will that one of these little ones be lost."[cxxi] It was the heavenly Father Who willed that Jesus remained hidden under St. Joseph's protection for thirty years before inaugurating His public ministry. Christ could say "[God] concealed me under the shadow of his hand, and He hath made me a polished arrow, in His quiver hath He hidden me."[cxxii] When you embrace the dark night of fatherhood, your child will become capable, after years of shrouding, of being a pure and radiant light in this darkened world.

## Go to Joseph for Hiddenness

St. Joseph is leading us up the Mount Calvary of fatherhood. This consecration journey will ultimately end with the death of our flesh, our selfishness. Yet from this death comes forth the resurrected man, the man of the Spirit. St. Joseph teaches us that we must flee from the Herods of this world. The desire for fortune, honor, and selfish gain must be exchanged for Christ. This is a tremendous sacrifice. Do you struggle with embracing the obscurity of fatherhood? Most men do. Yet by embracing the humble, secret way of fatherhood, you will be glorified by God. Turn to St. Joseph, who was a most hidden man, and ask him for the grace to embrace the hidden life of God the Father.

—*St. Joseph most hidden, pray for me.*

+ JMJ +

## Concluding Prayer

*St. Joseph, you were a hidden, humble father. In fact, your hidden fatherhood reflects the hidden fatherhood of God. Today you show me that fatherhood is to be hidden and humble. Yet, my flesh resists this truth. At times I am tempted to believe that I must make my presence known and glorify myself. Please obtain for me the grace to believe that my hidden fatherhood will glorify God, and in the end, that God will glorify this hidden father.*

*O Most Holy Blessed Virgin Mary, St. Joseph her most chaste spouse, by your union of wills and your most holy intercession, please obtain for me that the Holy Spirit conceive in me ever anew, ever more fully, Jesus Christ.*

*Litany of St. Joseph p. 171*

FULFILL YOUR SELECTED SPIRITUAL PRACTICES FROM
STAGE 5: COMMIT TO BUILDING YOUR DOMESTIC CHURCH
*See Custos Spiritual Practices Chart on pp. 8–9*

# Day 26

INVOCATION: ST. JOSEPH, TEACH ME HOW TO LOVE GOD ABOVE ALL THINGS

## GUARDIAN OF THE SOUL

*"Arise and take the child and his mother and go to the land of Israel, for those who sought the child's life are dead." Mt 2: 21-22*

St. Thomas Aquinas, commenting on this particular passage, noted that the Greek and Latin word "life" used in the phrase "those who sought the child's *life* are dead," actually means "soul."[cxxiii]

This indicates that God the Father commissioned St. Joseph with the incredible duty to provide for the material and temporal needs of Jesus, but more importantly, to be a guardian of His soul. Here we encounter a great mystery: God the Son needed a guardian for His human soul. We would benefit profoundly by meditating at length

+ JMJ +

upon this reality. For our purposes, it is enough to ask ourselves: if God the Son needed a human father to guard His soul, how much more ought we human fathers to guard our children's human soul?

The very life that constitutes the human person is his soul, which "is the innermost aspect of man, that which is the greatest value in him."[cxxiv] "The soul is the spiritual principle of the human being; the very 'form' of the body; for it is the soul that animates the body."[cxxv]

The body does not contain the soul, but rather the soul contains the body. The magnitude and reach of a man's soul extend far beyond his physical and temporal limits. Indeed, a man's soul may affect human beings in earth's most remote realms, while also spanning the ages.

The soul and body that constitute human nature are to be united by, and with, the Holy Spirit. Only in this way can a man be fully alive: if his soul is united to God's Spirit. Therefore, it is imperative that a father do all in his power to bring his child's soul into direct contact with the Spirit of God.

If this occurs, though the body of the child dies, the soul, animated by the Holy Spirit, lives on. It is this sanctified soul that will inform the shape, structure, power, and glory of its resurrected body. To prepare a child for his glorified, eternal state is a monumental task, a holy endeavor worthy of every father in every age.

While it is a father's duty to ensure that his child's body is protected and nurtured, more so is a father to diligently provide his child opportunities to be united to the Holy Spirit through occasions of worship, reception of the sacraments, moments of repentance, thanksgiving, joy that is the fruit of familial recreation, and constant prayer.

Your child's soul has priority over his body, and therefore it is your priority to nurture his soul by bringing it into union with God. If, however, you merely provide for your child's temporal needs while neglecting his spiritual soul, you have largely failed, and you will be held accountable.

"Is not life more than food, and the body more than clothes?"[cxxvi] "Therefore, if you, evil as you are, know how to give good gifts to your children, how much more will your heavenly Father give the Good Spirit to those who ask Him!"[cxxvii]

### Go to Joseph for Counsel

The purpose of every man is to live forever with God, and to help his family to heaven. Today's reflection prompts us to ask if this is our primary goal. Our efforts so often focus on providing for our family temporally. Yet, in the end, you can't take any possessions with you. St. Joseph knew that he was to protect the soul of Jesus. He shows us that more important than shelter, clothing, education, and success is the salvation of a child. Is raising your child for heaven your number-one goal? What ways do you struggle to make your child's salvation a priority? Share with St. Joseph these challenges and ask him for counsel.

—*St. Joseph, guardian of the soul of Jesus, pray for me.*

+ JMJ +

## Concluding Prayer

*S*t. Joseph, as I complete this fifth stage of my consecration, you ask me to evaluate my priorities. I fool myself into believing that God is my number-one priority. To make God my number-one priority is a great challenge for me. I feel torn in many different directions. Help me to love God more than I love myself. Help me to give myself totally to the one who gave Himself totally for me.

*O Most Holy Blessed Virgin Mary, St. Joseph her most chaste spouse, by your union of wills and your most holy intercession, please obtain for me that the Holy Spirit conceive in me ever anew, ever more fully, Jesus Christ.*

---

*Litany of St. Joseph p. 171*

---

FULFILL YOUR SELECTED SPIRITUAL PRACTICES FROM
STAGE 5: COMMIT TO BUILDING YOUR DOMESTIC CHURCH

*See Custos Spiritual Practices Chart on pp. 8–9*

Stage 6

# Live the Liturgical Life Days 27–30

As our consecration intensifies, we turn to St. Joseph to learn the importance of creating a continual connection between the liturgical life and our family. Therefore, with greater intention we commit ourselves to prayer, the Sacred Eucharist, and the celebration of feasts, solemnities. and holy days established by the Church. These practices allow Christ to become "fully lived" and "fully alive" in our family.

Suggested Spiritual Practices 27–30

# Day 27

INVOCATION: ST. JOSEPH, TEACH ME HOW TO SACRIFICE

## A United Front

*"And his parents were wont to go every year to Jerusalem at the Feast of the Passover." Lk 2: 41*

Besides the gift of faith, the single most beneficial, inspiring endowment that parents can impart to their children is a harmonious, united marriage. Indeed, if the couple are united to Christ in faith, more likely are they to impart faith in Christ to their child.

A house divided against itself shall not stand;[cxxviii] and if a marriage be divided, though it may endure bitterly this age, it will struggle to bear fruit in the age to come. The human father has been divinely endowed with the authority to establish his domestic church by initiating the dynamic of self-donation, which enables his marriage, his "house," to be united in God, lest division among its members occurs.

St. Joseph and the Blessed Virgin Mary had a profound union of wills—with one another, and together in God.[cxxix] The holy couple's

+ JMJ +

profound belief in God inspired them to trek to Jerusalem annually to celebrate the Feast of the Passover. The Passover is the summit and heart of the Jewish religion. It is a commemoration of God's deliverance of the Israelites—who were once enslaved to the Egyptians—by means of killing and eating a male, unblemished lamb and marking their residence with its blood. If an Israelite partook of the sacrificial lamb, the firstborn Jew and his family would be passed over by the angel of death.[cxxx]

Approximately fifteen centuries later, the Word became flesh in the person of Jesus Christ, who became the "Lamb of God,"[cxxxi] the lamb that "God Himself will provide."[cxxxii] It was this Lamb who instituted a new Passover, a new covenant in His blood, proclaiming that all "must eat His body and drink His blood, lest they have no life within them."[cxxxiii]

When the Christian partakes in the sacrificial Lamb of God, by eating His body, and being marked with His blood by drinking it, the angel of death passes over, and eternal life is granted to that individual. It is through communal Eucharistic worship that a family is saved.[cxxxiv]

To ensure that you and your wife, like St. Joseph and the Holy Virgin, become a couple who attends religiously and faithfully the Passover of Christ, it is imperative that you, as the head of your familial body and leader of your domestic church,[cxxxv] live what Christ proclaims in the Eucharistic Passover liturgy: "This is my body given for you."[cxxxvi]

A husband offers his body, his entire self to his wife, by striving to defeat lust in his heart, and by washing her in the Word—that is, by becoming a living, breathing expression of the Gospel of Christ, who "did not come to be served but to serve, and lay down His life as a ransom."[cxxxvii] Indeed, a husband is to love his wife as Christ loved the Church, by laying down his life for her.[cxxxviii] A husband must guard his wife's relationship with her Lord Jesus, by affording her times of prayer, spiritual retreat, and silence.

By living a husband's Passover spirituality—"This is my body given for you"[cxxxix]—his wife slowly, gradually is assured stability, security, trust, and refreshment not only in him, but more importantly, in Christ whom he represents.

By setting the pace of self-giving love in this way, a man leads by loving and loves by leading. Although human beings should never be manipulated or coerced to reciprocate acts of love, a man who consistently lives the Passover spirituality is inviting and encouraging his wife to enter the dance of reciprocal self-giving love. If this does occur, he and his wife will provide a united, harmonious, indivisible front to their children, and the angel of death will certainly pass over.

### Go to Joseph for the Ability to be Like Christ

Today, we are entering our second-to-last stage of our spiritual journey with St. Joseph. You are almost there. Though the distance is shorter, the climb is now steeper. St. Joseph and Mother Mary celebrated the Passover annually. The sacrifice of the Jewish liturgy became embodied in their marriage. St. Joseph invites you to take what you receive at Mass and bring it back into your marriage, into your home. Christ gives us Himself in the Eucharist while telling us that this is His body given up for us. What you receive, you must embody. And what you embody, you must give. Your daily actions must say to your wife and children, "This is my body given up for you."

—*St. Joseph, most sacrificial, pray for me.*

+ JMJ +

## Concluding Prayer

St. Joseph, your family was deeply connected with the Passover sacrifice. As I enter this sixth stage of my consecration, I sense that you are calling me to connect my family to the Mass by means of my self-sacrifice. This is a great calling. I cannot accomplish this on my own. Please obtain for me the grace to see my self-sacrifice as my ultimate end, and to accomplish it.

*O Most Holy Blessed Virgin Mary, St. Joseph her most chaste spouse, by your union of wills and your most holy intercession, please obtain for me that the Holy Spirit conceive in me ever anew, ever more fully, Jesus Christ.*

*Litany of St. Joseph p. 171*

**FULFILL YOUR SELECTED SPIRITUAL PRACTICES FROM STAGE 6: COMMIT TO LIVING THE LITURGICAL LIFE**
*See Custos Spiritual Practices Chart on pp. 8–9*

# Day 28

INVOCATION: ST. JOSEPH, TEACH ME HOW TO DISCIPLINE MY CHILD

## THE ASCENT

*"And when Jesus was twelve years old, they went up to Jerusalem according to the custom of the feast." Lk 2:43*

Submitting to the divine ordinance to sacrifice his "only son whom he loved," Abraham placed the wood on Isaac's back; "so they went both of them together," scaling Mount Moriah. It was in this moment, Isaac called out "Father," and Abraham responded tenderly, "Here I am."[cxl]

At the age of twelve, Jesus was initiated by St. Joseph into spiritual adulthood, "so they went both of them together,"[cxli] scaling the mountain in Jerusalem, to eventually offer sacrifice to the Lord in God's temple.

In a way similar to Abraham placing the wood on Isaac's back, one can imagine St. Joseph placing the sacrificial lamb on the back of his Son, who would become known as the Lamb of God. Christ certainly perceived, in this sacrificial lamb, an allegorical reflection of Himself and His ultimate human destiny: The Lamb of God who would take upon himself the sins of the world and the justice demanded of man's iniquities.

In a manner similar to Abraham and Isaac, Joseph ascends the mountain of sacrifice with his Son, Jesus, preparing Him to fulfill the divine ordinances of the Mosaic Law. St. Joseph placed the "weight" of sacrifice on the twelve-year-old boy, yet always with the tender fatherly encouragement of "Here I am." This "Here I am" granted the boy Jesus the confidence needed to ascend the mountain of the Lord.

Approximately twenty years later, Jesus, as a fulfillment of Isaac, would carry the wood on his back—alone. Only this time, the Son, Jesus, would be sacrificed on that wood. St. Joseph's fatherly "Here I am" echoed in the heart of Jesus, assuring Him of God the Father's faithful presence, "Here I am," which afforded Jesus the strength, the hope, and stamina to endure His bitter trial.

The day will arrive when your child must carry his own cross, and scale his or her own personal Moriah—and you will not be present to offer your "Here I am." Yet, just as Isaac recognized Abraham as his father, calling out to him "father," while Abraham prepared him for sacrifice, your child will come to love and respect you as you prepare him for his own personal Calvary.

Use the time that remains to teach your child how to carry the lamb, the cross, and most certainly your "Here I am" will echo in your child's heart, granting him the courage to confidently, trustingly, boldly cry out: "Father." It is then that your child will hear the still small voice of the Father: Here I am.

## Go to Joseph for Wisdom

No one desires to suffer. Yet, suffering will always exist. When confronted with suffering we have two choices: to avoid it or diminish its effects; or to embrace it and give it to God as a prayer for others. We need wisdom to know when to alleviate our children's pains and when to allow them to undergo suffering. If we always alleviate their pain, they will not become like Christ. If we never alleviate their pain, they will not know the Father's love. Wisdom is needed. Do you feel as if you are too hard on your children, or not hard enough? Ask St. Joseph for the grace to find the balance.

—*St. Joseph, help me to raise my child like you did: to become a person of sacrifice.*

### *Concluding Prayer*

*S*t. Joseph, yours was the duty to circumcise Jesus. Yours was the duty to work with Jesus. Though you loved Jesus, He experienced pain as coming from your hand. To raise my children to holiness is a wonderful and frightening thing. On one hand I can be too severe, and on the other, too lenient. Please obtain for me

+ JMJ +

*the wisdom to know when to ease my child's suffering and when to allow him to embrace and overcome it himself.*

*O Most Holy Blessed Virgin Mary, St. Joseph her most chaste spouse, by your union of wills and your most holy intercession, please obtain for me that the Holy Spirit conceive in me ever anew, ever more fully, Jesus Christ.*

*Litany of St. Joseph p. 171*

FULFILL YOUR SELECTED SPIRITUAL PRACTICES FROM
STAGE 6: COMMIT TO LIVING THE LITURGICAL LIFE
*See Custos Spiritual Practices Chart on pp. 8–9*

# Day 29

INVOCATION: ST. JOSEPH, TEACH ME HOW TO RETURN TO JESUS

## LOSING SIGHT OF JESUS

*"And after they had fulfilled the days, when they were returning, the boy remained in Jerusalem, and his parents did not know it."* Lk 2:44

After the Passover Feast, Mary and Joseph began their journey home to Nazareth. It was customary for female pilgrims, who walked slower and demanded more time for travel, to depart first on the journey, ahead of the male pilgrims, who would catch up with them by nightfall. Mary and Joseph had "come a day's journey before it occurred to them to look for [Jesus] among their relatives and acquaintances."[cxlii] But they did not find him.

Clearly, neither Mary nor Joseph committed any sin in taking their eyes off Jesus, but rather, each assumed that the boy was in

+ JMJ +

the other's caravan. Without sinning, we can lose sight of Jesus and assume He is with us.

Plagued by hurried busyness, we easily forget that God is present. We often attend Mass, worshipping Him, and upon leaving the church, we forget that He is abiding in our souls. His presence in our children too often passes unnoticed.

Life's circumstances assail and batter us, responsibilities and daily cares flood the mind, and at the day's end we may realize that though we began our day with Jesus, we have somehow forgotten or neglected His presence among us. We forget the real motive and reason for our existence. We forget the divine reason for why we are doing what we are doing. We reduce the supernatural outcome to merely natural goals. We forget that we are "laboring for Bread that does not perish"[cxliii] rather than perishable breads. We neglect to use our time to build an eternal heritage, and instead use the eternal heritage of God to build things in time.

Yet time is a bitter witness to the lost moments wherein we did not see Jesus, particularly in our children. Time holds no prejudice, but passes undaunted, regardless of a person's social strata or pedigree, only never to return. Time presses on while disregarding all who stand in its onward course. Only those who make use of it for God and His divine will give time an enduring quality. Indeed, we are to invest time in that which bears fruit in eternity. As St. John Vianney said, "The eyes of the world see no further than this life, as mine see no further than this wall when the church door is shut. The eyes of the Christian see deep into eternity."

When we inadvertently lose sight of Jesus and His eternity, immediately we must acknowledge our loss, grieve over this separation, and have a firm determination to search for Him until we find Him.

It is in the temple that Mary and Joseph found Jesus, and it is in the temple that you also will find our Lord: in the temple of the Church, waiting silently, patiently, in the Tabernacle; in your wife—if you have the eyes to see—and in the temple of your children, wherein God dwells.

Too often we do not see a child as Christ because we have not allowed ourselves to be Christ's child. It is the simple who see God in man. Indeed, "Blessed are the pure of heart for they shall see God,"[cxliv] and we may add "see God in their wives and children."

### Go to Joseph to Find Jesus

Why do you do what you do? When we forget that the reason we do what we do is for Jesus Christ, our life becomes shallow, meaningless. Jesus was the reason why St. Joseph did what he did. Joseph worked for Jesus, suffered for Jesus, sacrificed for Jesus, and gave up any form of self-preoccupation for Jesus. Have you accidently taken your eyes off the reason for your life? Go to Joseph. He knows how you feel. There was a moment when he accidently lost sight of Jesus. Ask him to obtain for you the desire to do everything for your Lord and Savior Jesus Christ.

—*St. Joseph, help me to find Jesus.*

+ JMJ +

## Concluding Prayer

St. Joseph, our journey together is rapidly closing. I hope that we never part. I have come to depend on your spiritual fatherhood. When you lost Jesus, you and Mary sought with great haste to find Him. I, too, have taken my eyes off Jesus. Yet, I am guilty because I have neglected to make Him my priority. Help me to find Jesus and never let Him go.

*O Most Holy Blessed Virgin Mary, St. Joseph her most chaste spouse, by your union of wills and your most holy intercession, please obtain for me that the Holy Spirit conceive in me ever anew, ever more fully, Jesus Christ.*

*Litany of St. Joseph p. 171*

FULFILL YOUR SELECTED SPIRITUAL PRACTICES FROM
STAGE 6: COMMIT TO LIVING THE LITURGICAL LIFE

*See Custos Spiritual Practices Chart on pp. 8–9*

# Day 30

INVOCATION: ST. JOSEPH, TEACH ME HOW TO REFLECT GOD THE FATHER

## SEEKING THE LOST CHILD

*"And not finding [Jesus] they returned to Jerusalem in search of him."* Lk 2:45

There is perhaps, for a father, no greater pain than the loss of a child; and if a father understands his mission properly (to raise his child to be a friend of Jesus and a saint of glory), nearly as crushing is a child who has rebelled against God.

This fatherly sadness acts as a window through which we are granted access to our Heavenly Father's heart and intention: that "not one of these little ones be lost";[cxlv] and again: fathers turn your hearts toward your children that in turning their hearts toward you they turn toward Me.[cxlvi]

+ JMJ +

If one could speak of God experiencing pain, there would exist no greater pain than the loss of one of His children to the devil's eternal tortures. This pain is channeled and dramatically expressed through the Son's execution. God the Father (through His Son) and God the Son are willing to endure the grief caused by the Cross, by the sins of mankind, for the purpose of sparing his children from the grief caused by eternal damnation.

Children will disappoint, rebel against, and betray us. They will unwittingly search for God in things, only to settle on things rather than God. It has been said that a father is only as happy as his least happy child. A true father will not be content until his child is content in the Father. God's divinity is wholly united to His Son in the Son's sufferings; and a father is united to his children in their sufferings, albeit less powerfully.

In our Lord's parable of the Prodigal Son,[cxlvii] we witness a son who has rebelled, disappointed, and betrayed the generosity of his father. He settled for his father's inheritance rather than settling in the love of his father. He abandoned his father's house, trekked to a foreign land—which to the Israelite meant exile—squandered his father's inheritance, and began to starve.

The story implies that the father waited anxiously, gazing with intense hope upon the horizon, longing for the return of his rebellious son; and when he caught sight of him in the distance, the father—without hesitation—dashed in frantic love to embrace him.

To comprehend the radical nature of this father's actions we must consider that a grown Middle-Eastern man of this time period and culture would avoid running so as not to appear immature, foolish, or weak. Yet, with great abandon, the father breaks all cultural norms, running to and embracing his fallen son—the son who betrayed him.

From the moment that St. Joseph realized he had lost sight of the sinless Jesus, he had a singular hope: to reunite with his Son. In his anxious, sorrowful search, St. Joseph realized that Jesus did not need Joseph to save him as much as Joseph needed Jesus to save him.

Regardless of your child's age, sinful past, current state, or geographical distance, your mission is to be a living representation of the heavenly Father by searching incessantly for, finding, and embracing your child. This is the way in which a child is assured of the Father's love: he has a father who runs out to embrace him continually. By acting in this manner, you will participate not only in your child's salvation, but also in the salvation of your own soul.

### Go to Joseph to Be Like God the Father

As we conclude this sixth stage let us consider that a child doesn't want to be accepted but rather chosen by his father. St. Joseph was a living symbol of God the Father to Jesus. You are a human icon of God the Father to your child. Do you go out of your way to show that you desire and choose your child? When you do this, you are convincing them that God the Father desires them, chooses them, and delights in them. Have you failed in being a living reflection of God the Father? We all have.

—*Let us turn to St. Joseph and ask him for the grace to be like him, a true icon of God the Father's love.*

+ JMJ +

## *Concluding Prayer*

*St. Joseph, you were a human reflection of the heavenly Father. I, too, am called to be a human icon of the divine Father. Yet, I am unlike you, and unlike God. I am selfish, and often fail to understand my child's heart. You teach me that to be like God the Father, I must seek out my child, choose my child, and convince my child of my love for him. Obtain for me the special grace to see and love my child as God loves my child.*

*O Most Holy Blessed Virgin Mary, St. Joseph her most chaste spouse, by your union of wills and your most holy intercession, please obtain for me that the Holy Spirit conceive in me ever anew, ever more fully, Jesus Christ.*

*Litany of St. Joseph p. 171*

FULFILL YOUR SELECTED SPIRITUAL PRACTICES FROM
STAGE 6: COMMIT TO LIVING THE LITURGICAL LIFE
*See Custos Spiritual Practices Chart on pp. 8–9*

Stage 7

# Work for God
# Days 31–33

As the end of our thirty-three period draws near, we learn from St. Joseph how to respect the goodness and divine purpose of work, while overcoming the temptation to use our labors to rob ourselves and God of communion with Him. Therefore we endeavor to surrender everything to God by turning to St. Joseph, model of laborers, and learn the art of placing our occupation at the service of our vocation.

Suggested Spiritual Practices 31–33

# Day 31

INVOCATION: ST. JOSEPH, TEACH ME HOW TO FORGIVE

## THE FATHER'S BUSINESS
*"Did you not know that I must be about my
Father's business?" Lk 2: 50*

The twelve-year-old Jesus, who had zealously entered spiritual adulthood according to Jewish custom, responded to his mother's plea, "Behold, in sorrow, *thy father* and I have been seeking thee."[cxlviii] Mary's words not only express her perplexity, but also reveal that St. Joseph was believed by Mary and Jesus to be a father in the most real and true sense.

Yet, Jesus' response, "Did you not know that I must be about my father's business," clarifies and defines the subordinate role of the human father to God the Father: the human father is at the service of the heavenly Father. He is a fatherly means to the child's end—

the heavenly Father; he must decrease that God may increase.[cxlix]

Indeed, as the child reaches and enters spiritual adulthood, his human father must decrease to ensure that the child's relationship with the heavenly Father increases. An overbearing human father can stunt the natural growth of his child's supernatural relationship with God the Father.

Too often fathers, and especially mothers, raise their children to retain their service, affection, and presence, while emotionally restraining the adult child from doing the Father's business. Such a parent fails to release his child to fulfill his great service to God. Such a father manipulates his child's choices, decisions, and future in order—subconscious or conscious—to live vicariously through a younger, more vibrant version of their idealistic self. Money, covering the cost of education, housing, or future inheritances are commonly used to manipulate a child into remaining in the service of his human father.

Though Jesus' response initially pierced the sensitive heart of St. Joseph, he eventually realized that Jesus must surpass his identification with his earthly father to be identified fully as the Son of the heavenly Father. St. Joseph realized that Jesus was no longer subject to "his business," but rather to his Father's business. It is a father's duty to help his child surpass his identification with his human father and to discover his identity as a child of God the Father.

In his accidental abandonment of his Son, Joseph abandoned himself to his Son's heavenly Father, hoping to be reunited with Jesus. Yet, in this reunion, St. Joseph discovered that he must further abandon his Son to the heavenly Father and His divine mission.

A father must be determined to allow his child to launch out and be about the Father's business. Often a child must wander and experience freedom before finding his way; a father must grant his child that freedom. It is imperative that a father refrain from expecting or demanding his child to return "to plow his temporal fields"; for a father cannot choose his child's future. God alone, in his sovereign knowledge, knows the path that the child must take. Who are you to know the mind of God?[cl]

Indeed, if you and your "business," that is, your motivations, decrease, and you set your child free to discover the heavenly Father's business, and your child returns to do you a service, you can be assured of your child's authentic love.

## Go to Joseph for Humility

As we enter the final stage of our journey with St. Joseph let us consider something rarely spoken of. After a father's children are grown and leave the home, he can feel a certain loneliness. Those children he loved nearly more than himself seem no longer to need him. They have lives of their own. We realize that perhaps we need our children as much as they needed us. Our Lord invites us to be like St. Joseph, and the Prodigal Father, and run out to our children. Let us seek them, visit them, and if necessary, ask for their forgiveness. Do you seek out your children? Have you any wrongs that need to be righted?

—*St. Joseph, humble father, pray for me.*

+ JMJ +

## Concluding Prayer

*St. Joseph, as we reach the last stage of our journey, I realize that after investing my labors and love in my children, they will eventually leave to live their own lives. This can be a cause of consternation. Yet, this allows me to understand the heart of God the Father, whose children often forget His generosity. Rather than feeling unneeded, obtain for me the courage to seek out my child as you sought Christ, and as the Father seeks His children.*

*O Most Holy Blessed Virgin Mary, St. Joseph her most chaste spouse,*
*by your union of wills and your most holy intercession, please obtain for me*
*that the Holy Spirit conceive in me ever anew, ever more fully, Jesus Christ.*

*Litany of St. Joseph p. 171*

FULFILL YOUR SELECTED SPIRITUAL PRACTICES FROM
STAGE 7: COMMIT TO WORK FOR GOD

*See Custos Spiritual Practices Chart on pp. 8–9*

# Day 32

INVOCATION: ST. JOSEPH, TEACH ME HOW TO BE PERSEVERE

## HOLY SUBMISSION

*"And [Jesus] went down with them and came to Nazareth and was subject to them." Lk 2: 51*

"For Jesus these were the hidden years, the years to which Luke refers after recounting the episode in the Temple... This 'submission' or obedience of Jesus in the house of Nazareth should be understood as a sharing in the work of Joseph. Work was the daily expression of love in the life of the Family of Nazareth."[cli]

Joseph, blessed with the presence of Jesus, blessed Jesus with an environment of mutual submission in Joseph the carpenter's workshop. The word "submission" can be interpreted as the act of participating in the mission of another. In the case of Jesus and Joseph, they joined in the mission of preparing Jesus for His sacrifice unto God, while preparing Joseph to release Jesus in pursuit of His sacrifice.

Joseph worked with Jesus and for Jesus, who worked with Joseph and for Joseph. Joseph by means of work trained Jesus in the art of self-offering, and was himself also trained in the same art. Such training presupposes the Son of God's willingness to offer all to His Father by working for, and with, His earthly father.

Working, sweating, conversing, sharing ideas and burdens, Joseph "prepared" his Son, by means of mutual submission, for His project of building the temple of sacrifice in His person. Within the humble carpenter's workshop, Joseph and Jesus crafted the cross of self-giving love by sharing themselves in their shared work. Because of this, work has been redeemed by Christ, making such work redemptive in Christ.[clii] Such familial work has been given the power by Christ to perfect us.

Work within the context of the family teaches a child to participate in sharing the burdens of others, which fosters communion with the other. Without familial work, a child often becomes slothful, neglectful of his talents, or worse, is unable to identify such talents and gifts in himself, failing to find meaning in his life. He becomes isolated in his lack of self-knowledge.

Familial work offers a context for children to participate in family life, and by using their abilities, gifts, and talents, to discover more of their particular identity. Within this context of familial work, the child can discover how to work selflessly rather than for gain. Such work enables the family to become a living representation of the Trinity's self-giving love rather than a worldly corporation that barters and exchanges goods and commodities for services rendered.

A father who serves his child will inevitably teach his child to serve. When a child learns this lesson, the burdens of life are shared, love is exchanged, talents and abilities are discovered, and the child learns to love like Christ. Submit then your fatherhood to God by crafting the cross of self-giving love with your child, and your child will learn to love and pursue the cross of sacrifice.

### Go to Joseph to Finish Well

Tomorrow we complete our consecration. What is God asking of us? By fulfilling this consecration, you are surrendering all your merits, good works, and labors to St. Joseph. St. Joseph presents you to the Blessed Mother. The two of them consecrate you totally to Jesus Christ. By doing this, you will be set apart for God and His Holy Will. Your life is not your own. Yet, by being a child of these holy parents, your life will be infinitely more than you can imagine. After Mary and Joseph found the lost Jesus in the temple, He returned with them to their home in Nazareth. This consecration demonstrates your desire to be raised by these holy parents.

—*St. Joseph, my spiritual father, pray for me.*

+ JMJ +

## Concluding Prayer

*St. Joseph, tomorrow my consecration journey will come to an end. Yet, you assure me that this is only the beginning. You assure me that I will be forever consecrated to you, to Mary, and ultimately to Jesus—to God. As Jesus returned to Nazareth after completing His Father's business, I, too, wish to enter the school of Nazareth and be raised to be a noble son of God.*

*O Most Holy Blessed Virgin Mary, St. Joseph her most chaste spouse, by your union of wills and your most holy intercession, please obtain for me that the Holy Spirit conceive in me ever anew, ever more fully, Jesus Christ.*

*Litany of St. Joseph p. 171*

FULFILL YOUR SELECTED SPIRITUAL PRACTICES FROM
STAGE 7: COMMIT TO WORK FOR GOD
*See Custos Spiritual Practices Chart on pp. 8–9*

# Day 33

INVOCATION: ST. JOSEPH, TEACH ME HOW TO LIVE THIS NEW LIFE

## SURVIVING SPIRITUAL FAMINE

*"And Jesus advanced in wisdom, age and grace before God and men."* Lk 2:52

It was in St. Joseph's house that Jesus flourished, advancing toward the full stature of sacrificial manhood.[cliii] The period of Jesus' preparation for His self-donation to the world is typologically prefigured in the epic account of the Old Testament patriarch, Joseph, son of Jacob.[cliv]

It was Joseph who by correctly interpreting visions in dreams, ascended to be appointed over Pharaoh's household; second only in his authority to Pharaoh himself. It was also by means of dreams that Joseph derived the foresight to gather grain into storehouses during seven years of plentiful harvest for

+ JMJ +

the purpose of sparing the people from starvation during the following seven years of famine.

When famine struck the land, the Middle-Eastern populace turned to Pharaoh, who commanded them, "Go to Joseph, what he says to you, do." [clv] By "going to Joseph," the multitudes received from his storehouses the grain from which they made bread that sustained them.

Our Lord Jesus, at the age of twelve, went down into St. Joseph's storehouse at Nazareth and during the following years of formation the "grain" of Jesus was formed into the "bread that would give life to the world." Today, modern man is suffering from a "famine of fatherhood," starving for authentic sacrificial leadership. To whom shall he turn for the Bread of Life? Our Lord himself asks, "Who then is the faithful and wise servant whom his master has set over his household to give them 'bread' at the proper time? Blessed is that servant, whom his master when he comes, finds so doing. Truly I say to you, he will set him over all his possessions."[clvi]

In another of our Lord's parables, Jesus also uses the phrase "master of the household," which in Latin is *paterfamilias*, or "father of the family." St. Joseph, son of Jacob, the just, faithful, and wise servant, who by means of receiving divine visions in dreams—with Mary—faithfully raised the grain of Jesus in his storehouse in Nazareth, to become the Bread of Life. Because of Joseph's faithfulness in this "small matter," God has given him the "greater responsibility" of being not only the "paterfamilias" of the Holy family, but also—as proclaimed by Pope Pius IX—the patron, protector, and *paterfamilias*, second only to Jesus and Mary, over the household of the universal Church.[clvii]

It appears that in our age of spiritual famine, Our Lord has ordained that all mankind, particularly fathers, have recourse to

St. Joseph, in union with Our Lady, entrusting themselves to his fatherly care. Those who do so will be given spiritual bread that nourishes them during times of spiritual famine. They will receive special graces, supernatural wisdom, and the virtue needed to raise families who become what his was—a holy family. Those who entrust themselves, their family, and their fatherhood to St. Joseph will learn from his timeless wisdom and ageless example, and be granted access to the Divine Mysteries contained in the hearts of Jesus and Mary; and be aided in their efforts to rise above temporal, natural, and material trials. Indeed, they will "seek the things that are above where Christ is seated at the right hand of the Father."[clviii] "Go to Joseph, what he says to you, do."[clix]

## Go to Joseph for a New Life in Christ

It is finished . . . actually it isn't. You have arrived at the top of the Mount Calvary of fatherhood. But there's more. Not only are you being transformed, but God is also transforming your relationships. For the last thirty-three days you have learned from St. Joseph how to live his spirituality. Today, you will forever consecrate yourself to God through Joseph in union with Mary as their son. This is a new beginning. A great beginning. Continue to follow St. Joseph by living the prayers and practices of this consecration. He and Mary will raise you to become like Christ. This is your ultimate goal: to be another Christ.

—*St. Joseph, my mentor, spiritual father, and my guide, I surrender my life to you.*

+ JMJ +

## Concluding Prayer

*S*t. Joseph, thank you for taking me as your student, your son. Thank you for teaching me your rule of life, your spirituality. Today, I surrender myself, all that I have and am, all my merits and good works, to you and to Mary. I choose to live your spirituality for the remainder of my days, that I may be a father like you, and that I may become a son like the Son of God. I am totally yours.

*O Most Holy Blessed Virgin Mary, St. Joseph her most chaste spouse, by your union of wills and your most holy intercession, please obtain for me that the Holy Spirit conceive in me ever anew, ever more fully, Jesus Christ.*

Litany of St. Joseph p. 171

FULFILL YOUR SELECTED SPIRITUAL PRACTICES FROM
STAGE 7: COMMIT TO WORK FOR GOD
*See Custos Spiritual Practices Chart on pp. 8-9*

+ JMJ +

# How to Make Your Consecration

*Today marks your adoption as a son of St. Joseph. He and the Blessed Virgin Mary will forever be your parents in the order of grace. From this day on, St. Joseph is your spiritual father and you are his spiritual son. By this act of total dependence and surrender to these parents, Mary and Joseph are consecrating you to Christ. Today, you have been set apart to be raised to the fullness of divine sonship. They will grant you intimacy with our Lord and Savior Jesus Christ. He will train you in the art of sacrificial responsibility, empowering you to become a father-king who is a living reflection of God our Father.*

*A most effective way to make your consecration is for you, at the end of the thirty-three days, to go to confession and Holy Communion with the intention of surrendering yourself completely to Jesus Christ through Mary and Joseph. After receiving Holy Communion pray the consecration prayer to St. Joseph. As an external sign of your dependence upon these holy parents, wear the Custos Brown Scapular.[1] Annually renew your consecration.*

---

1   The Custos Brown Scapular is a visual representation of our consecration and dependence upon Mary and St. Joseph. We pray: *O Most Holy Blessed Virgin Mary, O glorious St. Joseph her most chaste spouse, by your union of wills and your most holy intercession, consecrate me to God that the Holy Spirit conceive in me ever anew, ever more fully, Jesus Christ.* The front panel of the scapular represents the Blessed Mother. The back panel represents St. Joseph. We, in between the two, are the fruit of their spiritual union by the power of God's Holy Spirit. We are made into another Christ.

## My Consecration to St. Joseph

O St. Joseph predestined and chosen by God from among men, you received the glorious honor of being the chaste guardian of the Most Blessed Virgin Mary. Enflamed with divine love, you received her as your beloved wife, and through her, God bestowed upon you the most privileged distinction of being the virginal father of God the Son.

As a living reflection of the Heavenly Father, you protected the Christ Child from Herod, thus becoming the savior of the Savior. You accepted Jesus' humble submission to your fatherly authority and thus became the master of the Master. As a hidden king you conferred upon Jesus the Davidic kingship and thus became the king of the King of Kings. With untiring joy you labored to nurture the human soul and flesh of Jesus, giving bread to the Bread of Life.

Most gentle and generous father, look upon me, your indigent child, and see that I too need your care and protection. O chaste heart that burned with love for Jesus and Mary, teach me, your humble servant, to be devoted entirely to Mary and to worship the Lord Jesus with my entire being that I too may become a living reflection of God our Father.

O master of the interior life, you faithfully and promptly fulfilled the divine commands. Your humble obedience has elevated the vocation of fatherhood as a certain means to sublime sanctity and eternal glory. Desiring to follow your holy example, I embrace my vocation to be a most chaste husband, a living icon of God the Father, and a just guardian and guide that my family may become like yours, a Holy Family.

+ JMJ +

Therefore, most glorious and humble spiritual father, today before the heavenly host I surrender myself, my marriage, my fatherhood, my family, my labors, my merits, all that I am and have, unreservedly and totally to you, and consequently to Mary my Queen and most holy Mother, that you may always be my parents in the order of grace and that I may forever be your son. As you and Mary consecrated the Son of God to God the Father, consecrate me also, that I may be set apart for holy service to God Most High. I beseech you, as you prepared Christ for His ultimate sacrifice, prepare me also that I may attain the fullness of divine sonship.

Most humble, silent, and hidden father, I surrender all to you that my fatherhood may glorify God the Father of glory in this age and the age to come, forever without end, Amen.

_____  _____

Signature                                                                Date

+ JMJ +

# Prayers

### Litany to St. Joseph

Lord, have mercy.
Christ, have mercy.
Lord, have mercy.
Christ, hear us.
Christ, graciously hear us.
God, the Father of Heaven, **have mercy on us.**
God the Son, Redeemer of the world, **have mercy on us.**
God the Holy Spirit, **have mercy on us.**
Holy Trinity, One God, **have mercy on us.**
Holy Mary, **pray for us** (after each line)
Saint Joseph,
Renowned offspring of David,
Light of Patriarchs,
Spouse of the Mother of God,
Chaste guardian of the Virgin,
Foster-father of the Son of God,
Diligent protector of Christ,
Head of the Holy Family,
Joseph most just,
Joseph most chaste,

Joseph most prudent,
Joseph most strong,
Joseph most obedient,
Joseph most faithful,
Mirror of patience,
Lover of poverty,
Model of artisans,
Glory of home life,
Guardian of virgins,
Pillar of families,
Solace of the wretched,
Hope of the sick,
Patron of the dying,
Terror of demons,
Protector of Holy Church,
Exemplar of all fathers,

Lamb of God, who take away the sins of the world,
*Spare us, O Lord.*
Lamb of God, who takes away the sins of the world,
*Graciously hear us, O Lord.*
Lamb of God, who take away the sins of the world,
*Have mercy on us.*
V. He made him the lord of His house:
R. *And ruler of all His substance.*

Let us pray.

+ JMJ +

O God, who in Thine unspeakable providence didst vouchsafe to choose blessed Joseph to be the spouse of Thine own most holy Mother; and to be a father to you O Son of God: grant, we beseech Thee, that we may deserve to have him for our intercessor in heaven, whom we reverence as our defender on earth: who livest and reignest world without end. Amen.

## Consecration Prayer to St. Joseph

O St. Joseph predestined and chosen by God from among men, you received the glorious honor of being the chaste guardian of the Most Blessed Virgin Mary. Enflamed with divine love, you received her as your beloved wife, and through her, God bestowed upon you the most privileged distinction of being the virginal father of God the Son.

As a living reflection of the Heavenly Father, you protected the Christ Child from Herod, thus becoming the savior of the Savior. You accepted Jesus' humble submission to your fatherly authority and thus became the master of the Master. As a hidden king you conferred upon Jesus the Davidic kingship and thus became the king of the King of Kings. With untiring joy you labored to nurture the human soul and flesh of Jesus, giving bread to the Bread of Life.

Most gentle and generous father, look upon me, your indigent child, and see that I too need your care and protection. O chaste heart that burned with love for Jesus and Mary, teach me, your humble servant, to be devoted entirely to Mary and to worship the Lord Jesus with my entire being that I too may become a living reflection of God our Father.

O master of the interior life, you faithfully and promptly fulfilled the divine commands. Your humble obedience has elevated the vocation of fatherhood as a certain means to sublime sanctity and eternal glory. Desiring to follow your holy example, I embrace my vocation to be a most chaste husband, a living icon of God the Father, and a just guardian and guide that my family may become like yours, a Holy Family.

Therefore, most glorious and humble spiritual father, today before the heavenly host I surrender myself, my marriage, my fatherhood, my family, my labors, my merits, all that I am and have, unreservedly and totally to you, and consequently to Mary my Queen and most holy Mother, that you may always be my parents in the order of grace and that I may forever be your son. As you and Mary consecrated the Son of God to God the Father, consecrate me also, that I may be set apart for holy service to God most high. I beseech you, as you prepared Christ for His ultimate sacrifice, prepare me also that I may attain the fullness of divine sonship.

Most humble, silent, and hidden father, I surrender all to you that my fatherhood may glorify God the Father of glory in this age and the age to come, forever without end, Amen.

## Prayer to St. Joseph

O Saint Joseph, whose protection is so great, so strong, so prompt before the throne of God, I place in you all my interests and desires.

O Saint Joseph, do assist me by your powerful intercession, and obtain for me from your Divine Son all spiritual blessings, through

+ JMJ +

Jesus Christ, our Lord, so that, having engaged here below your heavenly power, I may offer my thanksgiving and homage to the most loving of Fathers.

O Saint Joseph, I never weary contemplating you and Jesus asleep in your arms; I dare not approach while He reposes near your heart. Press Him in my name and kiss his fine head for me and ask Him to return the kiss when I draw my dying breath.

Saint Joseph, patron of departed souls—pray for me. (Mention your intention.) Amen.

*The above prayer was found in the fiftieth year of our Lord and Savior Jesus Christ. In 1505 it was sent from the pope to Emperor Charles V, when he was going into battle. Whoever shall read this prayer or hear it, or keep it about themselves, shall never die a sudden death or be drowned, nor shall poison take effect on them; neither shall they fall into the hands of the enemy, or shall be burned in any fire or shall be overpowered in any battle. Say for nine mornings in a row for anything you may desire. It has never been known to fail.*

## Consecration Prayer to St. Joseph
## by St. Bernadine of Siena

O my beloved Saint Joseph, adopt me as thy child. Take charge of my salvation; watch over me day and night; preserve me from occasions of sin; obtain for me purity of body. Through thy intercession with Jesus, grant me a spirit of sacrifice, humility, self-denial, burning love of Jesus in the Blessed Sacrament, and a sweet and tender love for Mary, my mother. Saint Joseph, be with me living, be with me dying, and obtain for me a favorable judgment from Jesus, my merciful Savior. Amen.

### Prayer of St. Francis de Sales

Glorious St. Joseph, Spouse of Mary, grant us, we beseech thee, thy paternal protection, through the Heart of Jesus Christ. O Thou whose infinite power reaches out to all our needs, rendering possible for us that which is impossible, look upon the concerns of thy children with fatherly countenance. In the troubles and sorrows that afflict us, we have confident recourse to thee. Deign to take under thy loving protection this important and difficult endeavor, the cause of our worries, and dispose its success to the glory of God and to the benefit of His faithful servants. Amen.

### Prayer to Mary and Joseph

O Most Holy Blessed Virgin Mary, St. Joseph her most chaste spouse, my parents in the order of grace, I surrender myself to you. By your holy intercession consecrate me to our Lord Jesus that He may form me ever more fully into a son of God our Father. Amen.

### Short Form Prayer to Mary and Joseph

Holy Mary, Good St. Joseph, by the power of the Holy Spirit, may I be formed into another Christ. Amen.

+ JMJ +

## Short Form Consecration to Our Lady

Mother I am yours, now and forever, though you and with you, I want to belong, always and only to Jesus.

## Prayer to St. Joseph

St. Joseph, gentle and generous, make my heart like yours: little, silent, and hidden.

+ JMJ +

# Custos Theological Reflections

## A Letter from the Author

Over approximately the last two decades, universities, governments, churches, psychologists, and social scientists have compiled a mountain of data and research strongly supporting the idea that modern society is experiencing a famine of fatherhood, which has led to countless social and moral crises.[2] Collectively, both the secular and the religious have agreed that there is a crisis in masculine leadership. What we have yet to achieve is combining forces to develop a solution. Nearly every moral, social, cultural, or spiritual crisis begins with the crisis of fatherhood—not just manhood.[3]

---

2   Listed is a very small sampling of websites that outline the current fatherhood crisis and how it is shaping society: https://www.fatherhood.org/fatherhood-data-statistics; https://parentspluskids.com/blog/fatherhood-statistics-trends-and-analysis; http://fathers.com/statistics-and-research/the-extent-of-fatherlessness/; https://fatherhoodfactor.com/us-fatherless-statistics/; https://www.usatoday.com/story/news/nation-now/2017/06/13/why-dads-matter-according-science/377125001/.

3   An absent father in the household is the most important problem facing American families, 72.2% of Americans think (Fathering in America Poll, 1999: National Center for Fathering). The percentage of children without a father in the United States is 43% (US Census Bureau). Ninety percent of runaway and homeless children are from fatherless homes (National Institute of Justice). The percentage of rapists with rage that came from a fatherless home is 80% (National Institute of Justice). Seventy percent of minors housed in state facilities are from fatherless

Reverse this thought, and one can optimistically say that the rebuilding of society, the Church, the family, and marriages begins with virtuous, heroic, spiritual fatherhood.

It is not so much that we need men, as much as we need men who have traversed the rite of passage to become spiritual fathers.[4] The current crisis in the Catholic Church attests to this fact. You are either a boy trapped in a man's body, or a man who embodies fatherhood. Manhood is simply a stage between boyhood and fatherhood; you are either digressing or progressing to one or the other. It is a foregone conclusion is that society goes by way of the family and the family goes by way of the father; and if we want the world to change, we fathers must change for the better.

There exist many resources that help men, and there also exist some that aid men in becoming better fathers. While programs are beneficial, often they lack the ability to mentor a man effectively. The difficulty is that mentors, and those who are vulnerable

---

homes (US Dept of Justice, 1988). The rate of abuse and neglect in single-parent households is 27.3 children per thousand versus the rate of abuse and neglect in a two-parent household, which is 15.5 children per thousand (Center of Disease Control and Prevention). See also: https://parentspluskids.com/blog/fatherhood-statistics-trends-and-analysis; https://www.touchstonemag.com/archives/article.php?id=16-05-024-v; https://www.christianpost.com/news/fathers-key-to-their-childrens-faith.html

4   Spiritual fatherhood, though similar in some regards to biological fatherhood, is markedly different. Both the biological and spiritual father strive to be protectors and providers of their children's welfare. However, the spiritual father assumes the role and responsibility of being a "priest"-leader of his family. He has a singular goal: to spend himself for the spiritual salvation of his wife and children. Grace perfects nature, and therefore spiritual fatherhood in Christ perfects biological, natural fatherhood in every regard. Everything the spiritual father does is animated by his divine purpose to be a link between God the Father and his children. Therefore, whether he is a provider, protector, teacher, or exemplar, he seeks first the Kingdom of God in all matters.

+ JMJ +

enough to be mentored, are rare. Many men feel as though they are incapable of leading other men to the glory of fatherhood, while others are unwilling to admit that they need to be led. We all need to be mentored. We all need an example to follow. We all need to have a relationship with someone who has been victorious in overcoming evil; enduring trials, tests, tribulations, sufferings, and anxieties; and unshakably confronting the unknown. For those of us who are short on time or are afraid of joining a men's group or are unable to find a man who is willing to counsel and guide them: meet St. Joseph.

St. Joseph is like many of us: the least perfect member of his family;[5] silent—not much to say;[6] hidden—not very popular, and often not held in high esteem among his peers;[7] beset by the constant pressure to protect and provide for his family;[8] nevertheless called to lead in what often appeared to be an insurmountable situation. His heroic, strong example, experience, and person is worthy of our admiration. St. Joseph is a mentor worthy of following, and with whom we can have a profitable relationship.

5   Mary, the wife of St. Joseph, was full of grace (see Lk 1:28); and Jesus, the Son of God, was full of grace and truth (see Jn 1:14). Mary was a perfect creature, and Jesus is the God-man; therefore St. Joseph is not thought to be at the level of perfection of either our Lord Jesus or the Blessed Virgin Mary.
6   Not one word of St. Joseph's is recorded in Sacred Scripture. Yet, his silence speaks profoundly regarding fatherhood, God the Father, and what it means to be a faithful husband.
7   The people of our Lord's own village asked regarding Jesus: "Is this not the carpenter's son?" (Mt 13:55), which was a type of disparaging remark about Joseph and his character. They understood St. Joseph to be a mere carpenter incapable of raising a prodigy.
8   See Mt 2:16: Then Herod perceiving that he was deluded by the wise men, was exceeding angry; and sending killed all the men children that were in Bethlehem, and in all the borders thereof, from two years old and under, according to the time which he had diligently inquired of the wise men. See also Mt 2:20.

As Catholics we believe in the Communion of Saints. We believe that we are part of a collective whole that the Church identifies as the Body of Christ. A portion of that body is already experiencing the spoils of victory in the Fatherland. It is these victorious faithful—now fully divinized and animated by the Holy Spirit—whom God equips with grace and counsel, to aid the Church militant, while we endure our earthly pilgrimage. St. Joseph is not only among them but is ranked above them all[9]—save the Blessed Virgin Mary. St. Joseph is the patron of the Church, and the patron, example, and guide of all Christian fathers. His fatherhood to Christ surpassed being a foster father. He was a true father to Christ, and therefore he is the saint of, and for, fathers;[10]

9   Pope Pius IX decreed officially that St. Joseph is patron of the Catholic Church and that his festival, occurring on March 19, is to be celebrated as a double of the first class. (Pius IX Decree, Quemadmodum Deus, December 8, 1870, which gives him the highest honor of any creature, with the exception of the Immaculate Conception, Mary the Mother of God, Theotokos.) Therefore, by means of this position in the Church, he is ranked above all. As indicated by Pius X's words, "That even as Blessed Joseph, though being the father of Christ, 'became so much superior to all creatures as he inherited a more excellent name than they,' so by a decree of the Congregation of Rites, the public cultus of dulia should in future be granted him in the universal Church and in the sacred liturgy, second to the Blessed Mother of God and before all the saints; That, St. Joseph, to whom the protection of the Holy Family was committed, should be made, next to the Blessed Virgin, the primary patron of the universal Church."

10  St. Joseph is traditionally called "foster father'" of Jesus, or Jesus' adopted father. However, St. Joseph's fatherhood is more than that. According to St. Augustine: "Joseph is not to be denied as father of Christ under pretext that he had not generated Him, for Joseph would rightly be father even of a son who he had not generated from his wife, if he had adopted him from outside [his marriage]." "Luke did not call Mary Christ's sole parent; he had no hesitation in calling both His parents ... When, then, he records that Christ was born not of the act of Joseph but of Mary the Virgin, on what grounds does he call Joseph father unless we correctly understand that this was by the very bond of marriage." And again, "Was it not for another reason, namely, that Joseph was the father of Christ, who had been born

+ JMJ +

and he wants to have a personal relationship with you. He wants to lead you and all fathers to his Son, and his Son's Father—to ultimate glory.

This consecration is not simply to help us imitate St. Joseph, but to have an intimate relationship with him; and by entering into relationship with him, allow him to introduce us more deeply and fully to Mary, the Mother of God, and her Son, our Lord and Savior. In this way we move beyond imitation and begin to experience transformation.[11]

If you have not met St. Joseph, experienced his faithful friendship, his wise counsel, and heavenly support, then perhaps this consecration will help you forge a relationship with this most humble spiritual giant. May this spiritual father lead you to your heavenly Father and His Son, thus helping you to become like St. Joseph, a father on earth like the Father in heaven.

It is my sincere hope that an army of men will commit themselves to being consecrated to God through St. Joseph and begin to make the necessary changes that will overcome the world and participate in the salvation of souls for Christ.

---

of his wife—father so much more intimately than if He had been adopted from outside the marriage?" "Joseph's relationship to Jesus thus becomes something that far surpasses adoptive fatherhood." (Francis L Filas, S.J., Joseph and Jesus: A Theological Study of Their Relationship, p. 44.)

11   CCC 956: The intercession of the saints. "Being more closely united to Christ, those who dwell in heaven fix the whole Church more firmly in holiness... They do not cease to intercede with the Father for us, as they offer the merits which they acquired on earth through the one mediator between God and men, Christ Jesus . . . So, by their fraternal concern is our weakness greatly helped" [LG 49; cf. 1 Tim 2:5].

## Concerning the Act of Consecration

We have heard of individuals being consecrated to God, particularly in the biblical narrative. There are also individuals or groups who profess being consecrated to Mary, the Mother of God. As we proceed in discussing the act of being consecrated to God through St. Joseph, it will be beneficial to explain what consecration means.

The verb "to consecrate" can mean two different acts: First, as an act of the virtue of religion, one can consecrate oneself *only* to God (for example, a priest or religious sister). Second, as an act of the virtue of charity (divine *agape*), one can consecrate oneself to a human being. For example, a good mother could say: "I consecrated my life to my husband and my children."

Br. Hugh Mary, religious priest of the Congregation of St. John explains:

To be consecrated to God consists in belonging to Him willingly, exclusively, and entirely, soul and body, forever. As a consequence, the consecrated person renounces to be bound to a spouse by the Sacrament of Matrimony.

The other act is an act of the virtue of charity, the greatest theological virtue (*Cf.* 1 Cor 13:13), whereby one can consecrate oneself to a human being. We often speak about the "vows" pronounced by the spouse in the Sacrament of Matrimony.

This type of consecration is an act of divine love that implies a commitment whereby one promises—publicly or privately—to love the chosen person faithfully, all the days of his or her life. Such act of divine charity implies a perpetual commitment to act for the good and the joy of the chosen person, to respond promptly and with entire dedication to any desire or need the chosen person would have or express, etc. In brief, it is a perpetual bond in the order of love and charity.

To be consecrated to Mary and St. Joseph means to belong to them ("I am all yours"), in the order of supernatural grace, as children "belong" to their mother and father. We ask Mary and St. Joseph willingly to direct our life, to educate our affectivity, charity, faith, and hope, like parents would do for their children.

We entrust our person and activities to their care, promising to be attentive to their will and to act promptly upon it.

We want to belong to Mary and St. Joseph as the surest way to always accomplish the Father's will for us.[12]

## A Most Decisive Battle

*"No man can enter into the house of a strong man and rob him of his goods, unless he first bind the strong man, and then shall he plunder his house."* Mk 3:27.

Whether you believe it or not, you are at war. Sr. Lucia, one of the three visionaries who witnessed the apparitions of Our Lady of Fatima, said that the last battle between God and Satan will be over the family and marriage.[13] Why would the evil one spend his energies and resources for the purpose of assailing something so

---

12   Br. Hugh Mary, CSJ; approved by the Regional Censor of the Brothers of St. John on 2019-09-21.
13   Sr. Lucia dos Santos, one of the three Fatima visionaries, confided this to Cardinal Carlo Caffara.

apparently insignificant as the family, and as seemingly harmless as marriage?[14]

In the entirety of the created world these two social institutions are closest in proximity and similarity to God.[15] God is an eternal exchange of Persons; three divine Persons who are one in essence, each divine Person forever giving himself to the others.[16]

The Trinity's self-giving—the exchange of Persons—overflows into humanity perpetually, generously, in the forms of power, creativity, beauty, life, love, bliss, rapture, ecstasy, and fulfillment that will never end.[17] The experience of authentic joy, the creation

14 This satanic attack on the family was one of the primary reasons why Pope John Paul II wrote his letter to families: "Willed by God in the very act of creation, marriage and the family are interiorly ordained to fulfillment in Christ and have need of His graces in order to be healed from the wounds of sin and restored to their "beginning," that is, to full understanding and the full realization of God's plan. At a moment of history in which the family is the object of numerous forces that seek to destroy it or in some way to deform it, and aware that the well-being of society and her own good are intimately tied to the good of the family, the Church perceives in a more urgent and compelling way her mission of proclaiming to all people the plan of God for marriage and the family, ensuring their full vitality and human and Christian development, and thus contributing to the renewal of society and of the People of God" (Familiaris Consortio, November 22, 1981).

15 *"The Christian family is a communion of persons, a sign and image of the communion of the Father and the Son in the Holy Spirit" (CCC 2205).* And again, "When they become parents, spouses receive from God the gift of a new responsibility. Their parental love is called to become for the children the visible sign of the very love of God, 'from whom every family in heaven and on earth is named'" (Familiaris Consortio (November 22, 1981)|.

16 "God himself is an eternal exchange of love, Father, Son and Holy Spirit, and he has destined us to share in that exchange" (CCC 221).

17 "The Church cannot therefore be understood as the Mystical Body of Christ, as the sign of man's Covenant with God in Christ, or as the universal sacrament of salvation, unless we keep in mind the 'great mystery' involved in the creation of man as male and female and the vocation of both to conjugal love, to fatherhood and to motherhood. The 'great mystery,' which is the Church and humanity in Christ, does not exist apart from the 'great mystery' expressed in the 'one flesh'

of life, the witness of beauty, the fulfillment that comes from loving and being loved, is only found in relationship—more precisely, a relationship in which the two people give of themselves, one for the sake of the other. Marriage, then, has been divinely designed to be a living reflection of the Trinity.[18]

The Trinity is an eternal relationship whose attributes are distinction, unity, and fruitfulness—three distinct persons who are one in self-giving love, and from this union flows life and love to mankind.

God designed man to reflect, relive, and reveal the pattern of this divine self-giving love.[19] God creates a man and woman, two distinct persons, and by means of their complementarity He summons them to "complete" each other by means of their self-donation. Their union of souls and bodies is so fruitful that a third person is created, and from their marriage a family is born. Indeed, from marriage is born the image of the Trinity in the family.[20]

> (cf. Gen 2:24; Eph 5:31–32), that is, in the reality of marriage and the family" (Letter to Families Gratissimam Sane, February 2, 1994, John Paul II).
>
> 18 "The essence and role of the family are in the final analysis specified by love. Hence the family has the mission to guard, reveal and communicate love, and this is a living reflection of and a real sharing in God's love for humanity and the love of Christ the Lord for the Church his bride." This being the case, it is in the Holy Family, the original 'Church in miniature (Ecclesia domestica),' that every Christian family must be reflected. . . . It is therefore the prototype and example for all Christian families." (John Paul II, Redemptoris Custos, 7).
>
> 19 "The essence and role of the family are in the final analysis specified by love. Hence the family has the mission to guard, reveal and communicate love, and this is a living reflection of and a real sharing in God's love for humanity and the love of Christ the Lord for the Church his bride." This being the case, it is in the Holy Family, the original 'Church in miniature (Ecclesia domestica),' that every Christian family must be reflected. . . . It is therefore the prototype and example for all Christian families." (John Paul II, Redemptoris Custos, 7).
>
> 20 The Holy Family is the archetype and model of the human reflection of the Trinity. This family is the example for all families of what they are called to

Marriage and family, in its truest form, stands as an uncompromised reminder to the world of God's self-giving love, and that we are destined to partake in this love for all eternity. The family, then, is a beacon of hope, directing man to the shores of his eternal destiny.

Satan's intent, from the beginning, is to malign and redefine the sacramental sign of marriage and the family to ensure that it never resembles its Trinitarian identity and destiny.[21] His goal is nothing less than undermining or redefining the attributes of the Trinity in marriage and the family. The evil one accomplishes this by introducing every conceivable heretical ideology: Marxism, communism, hedonism, secularism, modernism, authoritarianism, homosexual

---

reflect and reveal. According to St. Francis de Sales, "There is, then, no doubt that St. Joseph was endowed with all the graces and all the gifts that were required for the care which the Eternal Father willed to give him of the temporal and domestic economy of our Lord, and of the guidance of His family. This was composed of only three persons, who represent to us the mystery of the most holy and most adorable Trinity; not that there is any comparison except with regard to our Lord, who is one of the Persons of the most Holy Trinity, for the others are creatures. But yet we may say that it is a Trinity on earth, which in a manner represents to us the most Holy Trinity: Mary, Jesus and Joseph; Joseph, Jesus and Mary; a Trinity marvelously estimable and worthy of being honored" (Conferences of St. Francis de Sales, Conference 19). And again, "The first witnesses of Christ's birth, the shepherds, found themselves not only before the Infant Jesus but also a small family: mother, father and newborn son. God had chosen to reveal himself by being born into a human family and the human family thus became an icon of God! God is the Trinity, he is a communion of love; so is the family despite all the differences that exist between the Mystery of God and his human creature, an expression that reflects the unfathomable Mystery of God as Love. In marriage the man and the woman, created in God's image, become 'one flesh' (Gen 2: 24), that is a communion of love that generates new life. The human family, in a certain sense, is an icon of the Trinity because of its interpersonal love and the fruitfulness of this love" (Pope Benedict XVI, Feast of the Holy Family, St. Peter's Square, Sunday, December 27, 2009).

21 See footnote 12, "numerous forces that seek to destroy [the family] or in some way deform it" (John Paul II).

+ JMJ +

"marriage," gender dysphoria, contraception, abortion, hypersexualism, materialism, contraception, divorce, adultery, pedophilia, ephebophilia, and the like; all conceived for the purpose of rupturing, redefining, and maligning marriage and the family.[22]

For example, contraception undermines the Trinity's fruitfulness. Homosexual "marriage" circumvents the Trinity's distinction of persons, which enables a couple to complement and complete each other. Divorce ruptures and divides the family, a symbol of Trinitarian love. Abortion destroys the fruitfulness of God's creativity.

Modern man scoffs at such proposals, dismissing them as archaic religiosity, naivety, negative pessimism soaked with prophetic doom and gloom. As long as a man receives a paycheck; is surrounded by climate-controlled comfort; numbed by streaming, stimulating forms of techno-entertainment; and comforted by ongoing pleasures, he struggles to perceive that he is amidst one of the most serious, costly, and damaging battles of all time.

Hence, materialism numbs mankind to the alarming reality that in his own backyard looms a disastrous immoral volcano that could erupt at any moment; and when he awakes from his drunken stupor of "comfortism," the safe and secure world he thought that his children would inherit may no longer be.

---

22 Pope John Paul hinted at this in his letter to the Christian Family in the Modern World: "Among the more troubling signs of this phenomenon, the Synod Fathers stressed the following, in particular: the spread of divorce and of recourse to a new union, even on the part of the faithful; the acceptance of purely civil marriage in contradiction to the vocation of the baptized to 'be married in the Lord,' the celebration of the marriage sacrament without living faith, but for other motives; the rejection of the moral norms that guide and promote the human and Christian exercise of sexuality in marriage" (Familiaris Consortio 7, November 22, 1981).

Society is overrun by hedonistic, pleasure-seeking individualism. The Church herself, particularly in her hierarchy, has been infested and influenced by a slathering of these ideologies, bringing her ability to be the harbinger of truth into question.[23]

The crisis at hand appears to be too cosmic, too catastrophic, too much for one man. And considering this, many men pretend that the battle for sanity and souls either does not exist, or that they are rendered powerless in the face of such evils. Consequently, Christian men are often paralyzed with fear, or succumb to numbing themselves with the day's temporal obligations or with distractions.

Unfortunately, very, very few men will admit that a severe crisis has fallen upon humanity; and of those who do, the majority of them remain on the sidelines, not knowing how to fight the enemy, or how to identify the weapons that will defeat this evil nemesis.

It is my sincere hope that this consecration will provide the weapons that empower us to be true disciples of Jesus Christ as fathers. The weapons this consecration aims to provide are: 1) a true knowledge of St. Joseph that inculcates respect and profound admiration for him and the vocation of fatherhood; 2) a means by which a person can "converse" with St. Joseph and take him as his mentor and guide so as to be Christ's disciple; 3) habitual daily practices and prayers that form a man into a true spiritual father.

---

23 "Through some fissure the smoke of Satan has entered the temple of God" (Pope St. Paul VI, 1972). And again, "To the injustice originating from sin—which has profoundly penetrated the structures of today's world—and often hindering the family's full realization of itself and of its fundamental rights, we must all set ourselves in opposition through a conversion of mind and heart, following Christ Crucified by denying our own selfishness: such a conversion cannot fail to have a beneficial and renewing influence even on the structures of society" (Familiaris Consortio 9, November 22, 1981, John Paul II).

+ JMJ +

## Binding the Strong Man

Though darkness looms heavy, and the storms of destruction rage on, there exists a reason for hope. God has not and will not abandon His people. God has prophetically foretold that the victory is ours if we but follow Him in the fight. Indeed, He has provided a remedy for our moral woes.

If the world is to be converted, the Church must be renewed; and if the Church is to be renewed, the micro domestic church that comprises the macro universal Church must be restored; and if the family is to be restored, marriage must be revitalized; and if marriage is to be revitalized, the man who is husband, father, and leader must take up his post as guardian of the mystery of the Trinity in the family. Though everything is set against him,[24] nevertheless this is his noble role and divinely ordained mission.

Indeed, society goes by way of the family because of its power to be a perpetual reminder of the Trinity; and the family goes by way of the human father (statistics, experience, and history testify to this truth).[25] If the world is to be converted and the Church renewed, fatherhood must be redeemed.

The evil one knows that the secret to redefining and maligning marriage and the family is to use the world, sin, and distractions to

---

[24] There is only one adventurer in the world . . . the father of a family. Even the most desperate adventurers are nothing compared to him. Everything is against him. Savagely organized against him. Everything turns and combines against him . . . Everything is against the father of a family, the paterfamilias, and consequently against the family. He alone is literally 'engaged' in the world, in the age. He alone is an adventurer" (Charles Péguy, French poet, 1908).

[25] See also Devin Schadt, Show Us the Father, 2016, appendix listing statistics and sources regarding fatherhood.

remove, paralyze, detain, and discourage the human father from living his unique vocation as protector, provider, and domestic priest, as guardian of the mystery of the Trinity in the family. Indeed, "no man can enter into the house of a strong man and rob him of his goods, unless he first bind the strong man, and then shall he plunder his house."[26] If the devil can successfully bind the strong man of the family, he can plunder the goods of his wife and children. If he can plunder the woman and child, society is all but abandoned, defenseless, and easily sifted by the devil's designs.

Unfortunately, fatherhood has become a lost art. Few understand the vital nature of the vocation of fatherhood; and fewer comprehend its unique role and essence; and even fewer embrace this heroic vocation and live it in such a way as to have lasting impact on the generations to come.

## St. Joseph Our Hope

More than ever, the human father needs a sure guide, a wise mentor, an experienced father, who in the face of horrific evils, has "raised" his family to sacrificial holiness.[27] The human father needs a father

---

26 Mk 3:27.
27 There is some question regarding the idea of Jesus (God the Son) being "raised" by Joseph. Here we cite several examples of teaching approved by the Church's Magisterium that discuss this: "It is no exaggeration to think that it was precisely from his 'father' Joseph that Jesus learned—at the human level—that steadfast interiority which is a presupposition of authentic justice" (Pope Benedict XVI). And again, "The growth of Jesus 'in wisdom and in stature, and in favor with God and man' (Lk 2:52) took place within the Holy Family under the eyes of Joseph, who had the important task of 'raising' Jesus, that is, feeding, clothing and educating him in the Law in a trade, in keeping with the duties of a father"

+ JMJ +

who will show him the way to correspond to Christ's command to be a perfect father on earth like the Father in heaven.[28]

Humanity is experiencing a universal famine of fatherhood and needs a father to feed them the experiential knowledge and wisdom of the full vision of fatherhood as exemplified by St. Joseph. St. Joseph "is the faithful and wise steward, whom his lord setteth over his family, to give them their measure of wheat in due season";[29] he is the father who can mentor, guide, and lead the human father to be a father on earth like the Father in heaven.

Although St. Joseph's renown was initially shrouded, over the last two thousand years his noble distinction and preeminence among men has gradually emerged.[30] His hiddenness serves as a fitting allegory for the current state of fatherhood. As St. Joseph has been eclipsed, in a similar way the modern father and his vital role has been eclipsed. Indeed, it seems that in our age God is revealing St. Joseph's vital role in the economy of salvation for the purpose

(Redemptoris Custos, John Paul II). And again, "The very purpose of the virginal union as determined by God was that it should prepare for our Lord's coming, should receive Him in its midst, and should rear Him to adult manhood" (Filas, Joseph and Jesus, p. 156).

28 Mt 5:48: "Be you therefore perfect, as also your heavenly Father is perfect." Our Lord calls us to "compare our fatherhood to the fatherhood of God: "If you then being evil, know how to give good gifts to your children: how much more will your Father who is in heaven, give good things to them that ask him?" (Mt 7:11).

29 Lk 12:42; the Roman Missal, Solemnity of St. Joseph, March 19, opening antiphon, uses this phrase to describe St. Joseph.

30 "Thus, then, it was that Joseph's vocation, according to the divine plan, called for his own obscuration during both the periods of the Hidden and of the Public Life—an obscuration that needed to be continued for a time even in the life of the Church. For belief in Christ's godhead and in Mary's virginal maternity had first to be established beyond all doubt against the heretics of the early centuries. With this in mind we shall better understand the reticence of the Gospels in their allusions to St. Joseph" (Francis L Filas, S.J., The Man Nearest to Christ: Nature and Historic Development of the Devotion to St. Joseph, p. 2).

of awakening mankind to the necessity of the human father.³¹

Pope Leo XIII proclaimed, "Fathers of families find in St. Joseph the best personification of paternal solicitude and vigilance."³² Indeed, St. Joseph was solicitous for his family's needs, while also being ever vigilant to defend his family from the evil one. According to Pope St. John Paul II, St. Joseph "is a perfect incarnation of fatherhood in the human, and at the same time, holy family."³³ Indeed, Joseph pursued sacrificial perfection and prepared his family to offer themselves in perfect sacrifice.

## The Purpose of This Consecration

The aim and purpose of this consecration is to help inspire men to "go to Joseph,"³⁴ discover in him this "perfect incarnation of fatherhood,"³⁵ and aspire to follow this sure guide.

The goal of this devotion is to entrust ourselves completely and

---

31  There is a notable movement toward elevating awareness of St. Joseph. Over the last century, numerous writings, books, programs, and apostolates have focused their work on the person and role of St. Joseph. Additionally, pontiffs have written about him and his name is now included in all Eucharistic prayers in the Sacred Liturgy: "On May 1, 2013, the Congregation for Divine Worship and the Discipline of the Sacraments promulgated the decree *Paternas vices* by the authority of the Supreme Pontiff, Pope Francis. The decree instructed that the name of Saint Joseph, Spouse of the Blessed Virgin Mary, be inserted into Eucharistic Prayers II, III, and IV. Already on November 13, 1962, Pope John XXIII had inserted the name of St. Joseph into the first Eucharistic Prayer (the Roman Canon), and that work was carried forward to the other three Eucharistic Prayers, initially by Pope Benedict XVI and confirmed by Pope Francis» (USCCB).
32  Quamquam Pluries: On Devotion to St. Joseph, Pope Leo XIII, 1889.
33  St. Joseph: Man of Trust, Pope John Paul II, General Audience; March 19, 1980.
34  See Gen 41:55.
35  St. Joseph: Man of Trust, Pope John Paul II; General Audience, March 19, 1980.

+ JMJ +

without reservation to the humble, protective care of St. Joseph, in the same manner that Mary and Jesus did. This is nothing new. Indeed, it is the very spirituality of the Catholic Church, which his holiness Pope Pius IX proclaimed on December 8, 1870, namely that St. Joseph is the patron (father) of the universal Roman Catholic Church,[36] entrusting her to his faithful care.

By consecrating ourselves to St. Joseph in this manner, God will draw us into the mysteries of Mary and Jesus, mysteries that this just guardian witnessed firsthand, mysteries that will inspire us to donate our lives and our fatherhood to Jesus, and ultimately to God the Father. In other words, St. Joseph will teach us how to love, protect, and guide our families by teaching us the way he defended, loved, and provided for his own family.

## The True Imitation of Christ

Some may have reservations regarding the need to be entrusted to St. Joseph for the purpose of being fully consecrated to Mary, the Mother of God, and ultimately—through them—to our Lord Jesus. Yet throughout our Lord's private life, but more precisely in the mystery of the Incarnation, our Lord Jesus submitted himself to Mary and Joseph's care.[37] The spiritual life of a Christian consists of nothing less than following Christ and participating in His life. The disciple is not greater than his master,[38] therefore we, being the

---

[36] Sacred Congregation of Rites, Decr. Quemadmodum Deus (December 8, 1870): p. 282.
[37] See Lk 2:51: "And he went down with them, and came to Nazareth, and was subject to them."
[38] See Mt 10:24.

Body of Christ, attempt to follow Christ, and doing what the Head of the Body did.

As in all spiritual matters we must look to the humanity of Christ and His example. Our Lord Jesus was not conceived by Mary outside of marriage. Only after Mary and Joseph were betrothed to one another (the betrothal was the first stage of Jewish marriage)[39] did the Word deign to become flesh in the Virgin's womb. One can say that Mary and Joseph's union of wills "drew down" the Word made flesh into their marriage.[40]

The Word was conceived and became flesh only within the context

---

39  "The root, 'to betroth,' from which the Talmudic word 'betrothal' is derived, must be taken in this sense, i.e., to contract an actual though incomplete marriage . . . In strict accordance with this sense the rabbinical law declares that the betrothal is equivalent to an actual marriage, and only to be dissolved by a formal divorce" (Filas, Joseph and Jesus, p. 17). And St. Augustine more forcefully states, "Here is another of [the heretics'] calumnies, 'Through Joseph,' they say, 'the generations of Christ are counted, and not through Mary. This should not have been through Joseph,' they say. Why not through Joseph? Was not Joseph Mary's husband? 'No,' they say. Who says so? For Scripture says on the authority of an angel that he was her husband" (Filas, Joseph and Jesus, p. 38).

40  "St. Joseph was the father and is the father of the Child Jesus because he lived in a virginal marriage with Mary the Mother of God. The marriage had its purpose as well as the justification for its existence in the Incarnation of the Son of God, which it served. In the sense we have explained, the Child Jesus was truly the offspring and fruit of the marriage" (Filas, Joseph and Jesus, p. 162). And again, regarding the idea of virginal fruitfulness, St. Ephrem applied the analogy of the palm tree to symbolize St. Joseph's role in the Incarnation of the Word. "St. Ephrem's idea is based on the legend that male palms are said to make female palm trees fruitful not by contact or by sharing of their substance, but by their mere shadow" (Filas, Joseph and Jesus, p. 28). "Thus, in the same way that they are called father although they do not generate, so is Joseph called father. " (St. Ephrem). And according to John Paul II, "Mary and Joseph . . . became the first witnesses of a fruitfulness different from that of the flesh, that is, of a fruitfulness of the Spirit: 'That which is conceived in her is of the Holy Spirit' (Mt 1:20)" (John Paul II, General Audiences; March 24, 31; April 7, 1982). In other words, both spouses' fiat to one another, and to God, was essential to God becoming flesh.

of holy matrimony—the union of Mary and Joseph—and God willed it as such.[41] Being that we are made brothers and sisters of Christ by the Holy Spirit, we can conclude that it is within the context of Mary and Joseph's spiritual union that we are conceived mystically by the Holy Spirit also; and formed by Christ's Spirit into other Christs. Regardless as to whether the faithful are aware of it, this spiritual dynamic has been occurring since the beginning of Christianity.

In the order of grace, the children of God are not only given a human, spiritual mother (Mary), but also a human, spiritual father (St. Joseph) who shares a union of wills with her.[42] By means of

---

41 "The Gospel does not say that he was conceived before the marriage pact. It implies that conception occurred later, when it states, 'When she had been betrothed.' Whatever happens after the marriage agreement, which is there called a betrothal, pertains in its entirety to marriage" (St. Albert the Great, quoted in Filas, Joseph and Jesus, p. 67). "The marriage of Mary and Joseph conceals within itself, at the same time, the mystery of the perfect communion of persons, of the man and woman in the conjugal pact, and also the mystery of that singular continence for the kingdom of heaven: a continence that served, in the history of salvation, the most perfect 'fruitfulness of the Holy Spirit.' Indeed, it was in a certain sense the absolute fullness of that spiritual fruitfulness since precisely in their marriage . . . there was realized the gift of the Incarnation" (John Paul II, General Audiences, March 24, 31, and April 7, 1982). Furthermore, according to George Foot Moore, "Betrothal was a formal act by which the woman became legally the man's wife; unfaithfulness on her part was adultery and punishable as such; if the relation was dissolved a bill of divorce was required. Some time elapsed after the bridegroom claimed the fulfillment of the agreement before the bride was taken to her husband's house and the marriage consummated. The term employed for betrothal, kiddushin, has religious associations; it is an act by which the woman is, so to speak, consecrated to her husband, set apart for him exclusively" (Filas, Joseph and Jesus, p. 17).

42 "Analyzing the nature of marriage, both St. Augustine and St. Thomas always identify it with an 'indivisible union of souls,' a '"union of hearts,' with 'consent.' These elements are found in an exemplary manner in the marriage of Mary and Joseph. At the culmination of the history of salvation, when God reveals his love for humanity through the gift of the Word, it is precisely the marriage of Mary and Joseph that brings to realization in full 'freedom' the 'spousal gift of self' in receiving and expressing such a love" (John Paul II, Redemptoris Custos, 7). Additionally,

our original human parents—a virginal couple—sin and death was birthed and transmitted to the human race.[43] By means of new parents in the order of grace—a virginal couple—grace and truth were conceived and given to mankind.[44]

In addition to this, approximately forty days after Jesus' birth, this holy couple presented the child Jesus in the temple to God the Father.[45] Mary and Joseph entrusted and consecrated Jesus to God the Father, Who in turn entrusted these holy parents with the mission to "raise" Him for the purpose of consecrating Himself as a sacrificial offering unto God.[46]

Similarly, our parents in the order of grace—Mary and Joseph—

---

this union of wills does not cease to exist in heaven. For "what therefore God hath joined together, let not man put asunder" (Mk 10:9); and "God's gifts and His call are irrevocable" (Rom 11:29). In other words, the elect, as they are drawn more deeply and fully into the eternal beatitude and mystery of the Trinity, become more unified than separated. If Mary and Joseph's marriage was a "perfect communion of persons" (John Paul II), and a "perfect union of wills" on earth (see St. Augustine and St. Thomas), we can logically conclude that this union is more perfected in heaven.

43  See Genesis 3; and also: "The harmony in which they had found themselves, thanks to original justice, is now destroyed: the control of the soul's spiritual faculties over the body is shattered; the union of man and woman becomes subject to tensions, their relations henceforth marked by lust and domination. Harmony with creation is broken: visible creation has become alien and hostile to man. Because of man, creation is now subject 'to its bondage to decay.' Finally, the consequence explicitly foretold for this disobedience will come true: man will 'return to the ground,' for out of it he was taken. Death makes its entrance into human history" (CCC 400).

44  "We see that at the beginning of the New Testament, as at the beginning of the Old, there is a married couple. But whereas Adam and Eve were the source of evil which was unleashed on the world, Joseph and Mary are the summit from which holiness spreads over all the earth. The Savior began the work of salvation by this virginal holy union, wherein is manifested his all-powerful will to purify and sanctify the family—that sanctuary and cradle of life" (Paul VI, Discourse, May 4, 1970).

45  See Lk 2:22: "And after the days of her purification, according to the law of Moses, were accomplished, they carried him to Jerusalem, to present him to the Lord: As it is written in the law of the Lord: Every male opening the womb shall be called holy to the Lord."

46  See footnote 21 regarding the idea of St. Joseph "raising" Jesus.

+ JMJ +

consecrate and present us to Jesus, in Jesus, with Jesus, and through Jesus to God the Father; and in turn God the Father entrusts these spiritual parents of the Christian human race with the task of raising children unto God for sacrifice.

This consecration is nothing less than the *Imitatio Christi* (Imitation of Christ) that inspires the faithful to embrace the reality even more fully that we are a part of the family of God.

This spirituality is embedded within the architectural psychology of the Church. Traditionally, the tabernacle that contains the Eucharistic Presence of the Lord Jesus is positioned in the center of the sanctuary, and flanking Christ's Eucharistic Presence, to the right and left, are the side altars of Mary and Joseph. The symbolism and significance expressed by this is inspiring and enlightening: The re-presentation of Jesus, in the most Holy Sacrament of the Eucharist, is in a certain sense "conceived" on the church's altar. The faithful receive grace and truth Himself through this holy couple's perpetual fiat to God. In addition to this, as we proceed to receive this great Sacrament, we present ourselves to God. Yet, more truly, we are presented[47] by our parents in the order of grace—Mary and Joseph, to

---

47 To some this idea of Mary and Joseph presenting a soul to God may seem artificial, unnecessary, or heretical, perhaps infringing upon the first commandment, "Thou shalt have no foreign Gods beside Me." However, to deny this spirituality is to reject the ministry of St. Paul, the Communion of Saints, the teaching of the Body of Christ, and the very generosity of God Himself. St. Paul assures the Christians of Colossae that he presents them as his spiritual children to Christ: "Whom [Jesus] we preach, admonishing every man, and teaching every man in all wisdom, that we may present every man perfect in Christ Jesus" (Col 1:28). St. Paul, in the following passages, conveys how he labors and strives to do this very thing: present them to God in Christ. An indispensable role of the minister, apostle, spiritual father or mother is to "present men in Christ Jesus to God." Due to the erroneous preaching regarding the role and nature of Christ Jesus, many non-Catholics wrongly believe that spiritual intercession, distribution of grace, and the like solely belong by right to Jesus, and He alone performs

Jesus, in Jesus, with Jesus, and through Jesus to our heavenly Father.

## Why Thirty-Three Days?

The duration of this devotion is thirty-three days. There exist other Marian forms of consecration that consist of a thirty-three-day devotion;[48] however, the length of this devotion was chosen for an altogether different reason than the traditional thirty-three years of Christ's life.

According to tradition, on October 13, 1884, after offering the

---

these ministerial functions. While it is true that by means of the Lord Jesus' Incarnation, death, and Resurrection He has won these rights, He also shares these spiritual gifts with his faithful. Precisely by means of Jesus' mediation as the God-man and minister of the New Covenant, all Christians share in Christ's mediation and intercession. To maintain the so-called Christian worldview that Christ alone mediates on behalf of man would logically lead one to believe that God greedily hoards his spiritual riches and refuses to share His power and glory with man. Our Lord Jesus, however, does not hoard his glory, but rather lavishes his spiritual riches upon his followers, allowing them to share in the spiritual functions that He has obtained from God the Father by means of His Incarnation, death, and Resurrection. Consider that our Lord has the power to heal, and yet He shared that same power with his apostles, as testified in the first five chapters of the book of Acts. Our Lord expelled demons, and yet has shared this power with His followers. He preached the Gospel and shares this gift with the faithful. He forgives sins and shares this power with His priests. He intercedes with God on behalf of men and shares also with men this ministry. He is the primary distributor of grace and yet shares this divine power with men so that they may become "generous distributors of God's manifold grace" (see 1 Peter 4:10). A true reading and understanding of Christ's Gospel grant us the certainty that Jesus who is Head of the Body (the members of the Church) desires that His body of believers participate in the sharing of grace and glory that flows from the Head. Jesus Christ who is the one mediator, or presenter of mankind to God the Father, desires that we participate in the presentation of our brothers in Him to God. In the order of grace, Mother Mary and St. Joseph, as parents of the baptized Body, are supreme under Christ in this ministry; for they presented Christ Himself unto God.

48  See St. Louis de Montfort, *Total Consecration*; Fr. Michael Gaitley, *33 Days to Morning Glory*.

+ JMJ +

Holy Sacrifice of the Mass, Pope Leo XIII collapsed and appeared to have received some type of vision. It has been recounted that during this moment, the holy pontiff received a locution in which he heard Satan addressing God, demanding that he could destroy the Church if given more power and one hundred years.

Ironically, thirty-three years to the date of this event, God provided His response and remedy to Satan's agenda. On October 13, 1917, Our Lady of Fatima appeared to three peasant children for the sixth time, while approximately seventy thousand inquisitive pilgrims looked on in expectation for the miracle promised in an earlier apparition of Our Lady. During the apparition, the sun began to "dance" in the sky, moving radically, and appeared to descend suddenly upon the onlookers. Simultaneously, the visionaries witnessed St. Joseph and the child Jesus—whom he was holding—bless the world. At the moment of their blessing, the sun returned to its original position in the sky and disaster was averted.[49] Afterward, Our Lady appeared together with St. Joseph and Jesus, forming the Holy Family.[50]

---

49  Secular sources such as Lisbon papers O Dia and O Secula, who skeptically criticized the visionaries prior to the miracle, reported that a miraculous event had indeed occurred. O Dia wrote, "The silver sun . . . was seen to whirl and turn in the circle of broken clouds. A cry went up from every mouth and the people fell on their knees on the muddy ground . . . The light turned a beautiful blue as if it had come through the stained-glass windows of a cathedral and spread itself over the people who knelt with outstretched hands. The blue faded slowly and then the light seemed to pass through yellow glass . . . People wept and prayed with uncovered heads in the presence of the miracle they had awaited. The seconds seemed like hours, so vivid were they/." O Dia. See also: https://catholicherald.co.uk/issues/october-13th-2017/how-the-miracle-of-the-sun-dazzled-the-sceptics.
50  For a comprehensive recounting of the apparitions of Our Lady of Fatima see also: Sister Lucia, Fatima in Lucia's Own Words, 1976; and Calls from the Message of Fatima, 2000.

The significance and symbolism of this event cannot be overstated. Our Lady of Fatima's core message was "In the end my Immaculate Heart will triumph." How will her Immaculate Heart triumph over the evil one? It appears that the Queen of Heaven is saying that fatherhood as exemplified by St. Joseph is a primary weapon in overcoming degeneration, disaster, and war. Indeed, when a father follows the holy example of St. Joseph, his family will be united as a holy family.

It is as though Mary is saying, "I am not sufficient. The human family needs not only a human mother, but also a human father, who together will provide the timeless example and ageless wisdom needed to raise a family holy unto God." Yet, this holy couple offers far more than an example worthy of imitation. These holy parents transmit all graces to Christ's body, His Church. Just as the Word became incarnate and was given to the world by means of Mary and Joseph's holy marriage, so also, God's grace is perpetually transmitted to us through them; for the gift and the call of God are irrevocable.[51]

It is as if Mary is offering the secret to converting society, renewing the Church, restoring the family, and revitalizing marriage: Husbands and fathers, go to Joseph, what he says to you, do.[52] Learn from him how to become a father on earth like the Father in heaven. Learn from him how to set the pace of self-giving love for your families. Receive St. Joseph as your spiritual mentor, guide, father, and friend. He will show you the certain and true path to fatherly glory. In union with my motherly intercession, he will

---

51 See Rom 11:29.
52 See Gen 41:55.

+ JMJ +

obtain for you all things necessary to become a sacrificial leader.[53] He will teach you how to trust and triumph amidst trials, tests, and tribulations. He will show you how to love me, your Mother, and Jesus your Savior.

[53] "I took for my advocate and master the glorious St. Joseph, and I recommended myself much to him; for I saw clearly that where my honor and the loss of my soul were concerned, my father and master delivered me from that danger, as well as from others still greater, and this with more advantage than I could desire myself. Up to this time I cannot remember having asked him for anything which he did not obtain, I am quite amazed when I consider the great favors our Lord has shown me through the intercession of this blessed saint, and the many dangers both of body and soul from which he has delivered me. It seems that to other saints our Lord has given power to succor us in only one kind of necessity; but this glorious saint, I know by my experience, assists us in all kinds of necessities; hence our Lord, it appears, when on earth (for he was called His father; and being, as it were, His guardian, he could command Him), so now in Heaven He grants him whatever he asks. This truth many others also have experienced who have recommended themselves to him by my desire. Many are now devoted to him, and I myself have fresh experience of his power . . . Would that I could persuade all men to be devout to this glorious saint, by reason of the great experience I have had of the blessings he obtains from God. I have never known anyone who was truly devoted to him, who performed particular devotions in his honor, that did not advance more in virtue, for he assists in a special manner those souls who recommend themselves to him. During many years I was accustomed to ask some favor of him, and I remember that it was always granted; and if sometimes my petition had something wrong about it, he rectified it for my greater good . . . I only request, for the love of God, that whoever will not believe me will prove the truth of what I say, for he will see by experience how great a blessing it is to recommend oneself to this glorious patriarch and to be devout to him. Those persons who are given to prayer should be ever devoted to him, for I know not how they can think of the Queen of Angels—at the time when she suffered so much on account of the child Jesus—and not give thanks to St. Joseph for the assistance he gave them. Whoever wants a master to instruct him how to pray, let him take this glorious saint for his guide and he will not lose his way" (St. Teresa of Avila, Autobiography of St. Teresa of Avila, Chapter VI). And again, "Some Saints are privileged to extend to us their patronage with particular efficacy in certain needs, but not in others; but our holy patron St. Joseph has the power to assist us in all cases, in every necessity, in every undertaking" (St. Thomas Aquinas).

## God's Intention and Plan

Indeed, centuries prior to this supernatural event, God through the prophet Malachi provided His intention and plan to save the world from disaster: "Fathers turn your hearts toward your children, so that children will turn their hearts toward their fathers."[54] When fathers turn their attention, affirmation, and love upon their children, their children will sense the heavenly Father's love through their human fathers, and begin to entrust themselves with confidence and trust in the heavenly Father. Fatherhood is primary to God's plan for the restoration and redemption of mankind. Our Lady of Fatima appears to be directing humanity to the exemplar model father who gazed lovingly upon his son Jesus, and in turn, Jesus entrusted himself to Joseph, and ultimately to God the Father.

By entrusting ourselves fully to St. Joseph and his patronage, we will more fully surrender ourselves to Mary, receiving her fully as our true Mother; and by means of their holy union of wills, we will consecrate ourselves to our Lord and Savior Jesus in the very manner that He gave Himself to us. The aim and goal of this consecration is to inspire men to entrust their fatherhood and families to St. Joseph; and by doing so, receive particular and powerful graces that will aid them in achieving great sanctity, glorifying God in this age and the age to come. By means of this devotion, one can truly become a child of St. Joseph and Holy Mary's virginal union.[55] By

---

54 Mal 4:5–6.
55 Commenting on the virginal character of Mary and Joseph's marriage, St. Augustine remarks: "Because of this holy virginal marriage with Christ's mother, Joseph merited to be called the very father of Christ" (St. Augustine, quoted in Filas, Joseph and Jesus, p. 45).

+ JMJ +

means of their intercession before God, a man can be formed into another Christ who lives for the praise of God's glory.

## The Structure of this Consecration

Our consecration to St. Joseph can be described more explicitly as entrusting ourselves completely to St. Joseph's care that we may live in spiritual communion with Mary, and by placing ourselves in these holy parents' care, they may obtain for us perpetually the gift of the Holy Spirit, who will continually form Christ anew in us; while also presenting us in Christ, through Christ, and with Christ to the Trinity.

The format of this consecration is comprised of thirty-three days of concise reflections (one per day) that are based strictly on the scriptural passages that apply directly to St. Joseph and his life, and that span from the moment that we encounter this "just man"[56] in Matthew's genealogy, to the twelve-year-old Jesus' obedient submission in "going down" with his parents to their home in Nazareth.[57]

Each reflection enables us to meditate on St. Joseph's vocational path; his supreme character; his glorious virtues; his love for and

---

56   See Mt 1:19.
57   Many books about St. Joseph exist. Typically, devotional-style books written about St. Joseph use the method of beginning with or emphasizing a particular virtue, a holy action, or a Christian ideal, and then grafting on St. Joseph as an example who confirms and validates the topic at hand This work, however, is exegetical in its approach. The Greek word for "exegesis," exēgeisthai, is defined as explaining or interpreting, from ex- + hēgeisthai, "to lead." In other words, we will always begin with the divinely inspired Sacred Scripture and working from that foundation we will be led to the meaning of the text, which will afford us a truer and clearer vision of St. Joseph.

fidelity to God, Mary, and the child Jesus, in a chronological, step-by-step manner.

Prior to each reflection, a sentence, or a phrase from a sentence, or a portion of a phrase is cited, indicating a moment of Joseph's life that will be expounded upon briefly. The purpose behind this methodology is to enable one to pause, ponder, and spiritually walk with greater intention and focus in the shadow of this holy father.[58] Each reflection concludes with a prayer to St. Joseph, requesting him to obtain from Christ a particular grace or virtue.

The consecration is segmented into seven stages. Each stage has a set of daily practices that apply specifically to the theme of that stage, with the aim of making this spirituality practical. Each stage's practices build upon the previous stage's practices so that by the completion of this thirty-three day consecration, you will have developed virtuous habits that will reshape your spiritual life and will have tremendous impact on your vocation and family. Each day, as a sign of personal devotion to St. Joseph, the Litany of St. Joseph should be prayed.

The thirty-three days conclude with the participant confessing his sins to a Catholic priest: receiving the Holy Sacrament of the Eucharist, and afterward praying the consecration prayer to St. Joseph.

The exterior form of this practice consists in a participant enthroning St. Joseph as "master of his house, and ruler of all his

---

58 The Fathers of St. Joseph proclaim and live St. Joseph's spirituality, which consists of his four pillars: embrace silence, embrace woman, embrace the child, embrace charitable authority. Though each reflection certainly touches upon one of the four pillars of St. Joseph's spirituality, they are not categorized according to these four pillars. This work avoids such categorization for the purpose of maintaining the chronological unfolding of Josephs' life as expressed in the Sacred Scripture, thus helping us to walk his vocational path in the order that St. Joseph experienced it.

+ JMJ +

possessions,"[59] by having St. Joseph's image hung in a place of honor in his home, and by being clothed in the Custos Brown Scapular, while striving to live his spirituality, which consists of St. Joseph's four pillars.

## Prayers and Practices[60]

Though a man may make a spirituality, a spirituality does not make a man. Though a man may attempt to use a spirituality to transform himself into a saint, it is God who uses a spirituality to transform a man into a saint. To be clear, neither a spirituality nor a man can make a man a saint; only God can make the man into a saint. It is important to keep this truth in mind during the course of this consecration; for if we begin to believe that by performing and successfully completing our spiritual practices[61] we are climbing the mountain of sainthood ourselves—by our own doing—we are certain to fall from the precipice of pride.

Too often, a person can mistakenly approach the call to sanctity as merely a process of identifying, embracing, and fulfilling active sacrifices, practices, and mortifications. This view reduces the spiritual life to a formulaic methodology based on what the person does, rather than what God is doing in the person.

If the spiritual life, the call to sanctity, can be expressed by a loosely outlined formula (which, ultimately, it cannot), it would

---

59 See Psalm 105:21, and the Litany of St. Joseph.
60 The Spiritual Practices chart outlining the seven stages and the practices associated with each stage is located on pp. 8–9. Detailed explanations of the Prayers and Practices begin on p. 213.
61 The list of Spiritual Practices and their explanations begins on p. 213.

consist of a person engaging and offering active sacrifices to God, in addition to receiving and accepting and offering in return to God those passive sacrifices and sufferings that God wills. Both active sacrifices and passive sufferings are necessary for one's sanctity.

If the spiritual journey of a man is to be likened to the work of a gardener, then active sacrifices can be compared to the toil and labor demanded of the gardener to prepare the soil. Indeed, this is his primary duty: to prepare the soil by means of his active sacrifices—those he has personally chosen for himself. Such active sacrifices are not the seed, nor the water, nor the sun, or that which makes the seed grow. His active sacrifices till and open the soil to receive the seed, then after the seed is planted, his active sacrifices continue to serve as fertilizer that aids the plant's growth. Nevertheless, all such labor should be understood as nothing more than fertilizer.

The fundamental difference between active and passive sacrifices is that active sacrifices are those which we choose for ourselves. We determine whether we take on such sufferings and mortifications. We determine the intensity, the duration, the type, and the level of the mortification; and when it moves even a hair beyond what we believe we can handle, we discontinue the sacrifice or lessen the intensity of it. In other words, active sacrifices are completely under our control.

Passive sufferings and sacrifices are those which God chooses for us. He determines the intensity, the type, the level, and the duration. In this case, we have very little—if any—control over the situation. Indeed, this lack of control, and lack of knowledge as to when the suffering will cease, and what areas of our life it will affect, only intensify the suffering.

+ JMJ +

Passive sufferings are like a mountain of sanctity, with its sharp stones, perilous precipices, steep climbs. We did not make the mountain—God did; and we did not make the difficulties we encounter while climbing the mountain—God allows such challenges. Nevertheless, we climb. Active sacrifices can be likened to the trekking poles that assist a man in his climb. They are not the mountain but strengthen and steady the man as he proceeds with the climb.

Between these two sacrifices is a vast gulf, likened to the difference between a man's works, which are like filthy rags, and God's action in the soul, which is like Christ transforming water into wine. In fact, our sacrifices are like the water, and passive sufferings, if embraced, are like Christ's act of transforming the water into wine. Both are needed; yet only God can provide the transformation.

Considering this, the spiritual practices of this consecration are not to be misunderstood as a "checklist" that will make one holy. In fact, our journey will demand that we exercise greater faith in what God is doing in us, and less reliance on our own doing. We will use this consecration's prayers and practices to till the hardened soil of our hearts. By means of this cultivation, the soil of our hearts will be better prepared to receive the seed of the Holy Spirit, which alone can transform us; giving us a heart devoted to God.

During the thirty-three days, we climb the mountain of sanctity, following in the footsteps of our spiritual father and guide, St. Joseph, who will show us the path to become a true follower of Christ by means of embracing our fatherly vocation. Indeed, our vocation as a husband and father is the path to the pinnacle of this mountain.

## Motivations Matter

Motives matter. The underlying "why" behind what we do is often more important than the outcome of what we do. A man may be well known because of his apparent charity; yet if the motive behind his acts of charity is to use charity to become lauded, then it is not charity per se, but vanity. Similarly, one can use prayer, fasting, and almsgiving—all good in themselves—to glorify oneself rather than for the purpose of glorifying God. If a man glorifies God, God cannot help but glorify a man; but he ought to let God determine how he is glorified.

The motivation behind the spiritual practices of this consecration is not as much about us as it is about God and others. The man who fasts for others may consequently have the added benefit of losing weight; yet his primary motive was not to lose weight but to "gain" grace for others. If the motive behind these daily practices is love of God and love of neighbor, the participant will also benefit greatly from these practices, for God will not be outdone in generosity.

Our motivation is fourfold: first to repent and do penance for our sins; second as an act of thanksgiving for Christ's sacrifice of Himself for our sins and His redemptive work in us; third, as a priestly sacrifice for the spiritual and temporal well-being and salvation of others; and last, to grow in love of and communion with God. Over the course of thirty-three days, we offer our daily practices as an act of penance for those times when we have neglected our vocational responsibility; as an act of thanksgiving to God for our marriage and family; as an offering for the salvation and sanctification of our wives and children; and for a more profound personal communion with God.

+ JMJ +

These practices are not be viewed as arbitrary impositions, but rather as outgrowths of the four pillars that constitute St. Joseph's spirituality: embrace silence, embrace woman, embrace the child, and embrace charitable authority. These practices are not to be perceived as a harsh rule, nevertheless one ought to strive to complete them to the best of one's ability and state of life. By doing so, your life will be built upon the four pillars of St. Joseph's spirituality. Each stage's practices build upon the previous stage's practices, so that by the completion of the consecration you will have implemented a way of life that continually cultivates the soil of your heart to receive the passive sufferings that God will demand of you to forge you into a saint.[62] Though it may appear that God asks much of you, be not dismayed or disheartened; the spiritual benefits that God grants to a man who lives this spirituality are numerous, effective, and transformative. God is calling you to be a saint, and your vocation is the path by which you are to climb this mountain.

---

62  The Spiritual Practices Chart is located on pp. 8–9.

+ JMJ +

# The Thirty-Three Spiritual Practices

### 1. Daily Morning Offering

Upon waking, prior to viewing any emails or texts—or doing anything else—drop down to the floor and surrender yourself, and your day, to God. By previewing or viewing texts or emails, listening to podcasts, music, or the news prior to your morning offering, you will have surrendered to the world instead of giving your first fruits to God. In addition, when possible, make your morning offering on your knees and with your head bowed down to the floor. The reason for this is that your body expresses what your soul believes. By kneeling, or praying in a prostrate position, your body express that you are spiritually submitting and surrendering your soul to God's Holy Will. Your morning offering consists of offering to God the Father all that you are and have, through, with, and in His Son, Jesus Christ; imploring the Holy Spirit to animate and direct you throughout the day; and offering yourself to Jesus Christ in the manner by which He came to us: through the union of the Virgin Mary and St. Joseph. The purpose behind your morning offering is simply "reporting for duty," acknowledging to God your worship of Him and your readiness to serve Him wholeheartedly.

**Sample morning offering:** Heavenly Father, I offer you my day; all that I am and have to you—spiritual, temporal, physical, thoughts, memory, will, and good actions—through, with, and in your Son, our Lord, Jesus Christ, in union with all the Masses offered throughout the world, for the conversion of sinners, for the reparation of sins, for the holy souls in purgatory to be drawn into your Divine Light, and most of all, for the love of Thee, My God. Lord Jesus. I do not presume to come to you alone; but rather approach you in the way You came to us, through the holy union of the Blessed Virgin and St. Joseph, her chaste spouse. Holy Mary, good St. Joseph, by your union of wills and your intercession before God, obtain for me the gift of the Holy Spirit, that our Lord Jesus may be conceived ever anew and ever more fully in me. My guardian angel intercede for me.

## 2. Daily Litany of St. Joseph

The litany of St. Joseph is a way to quickly offer St. Joseph honor, while also becoming acquainted with his gifts and virtues, which we ought to imitate. See the Litany of St. Joseph on p. 171.

## 3. Daily Examination of Conscience

Toward the end of day, prior to retiring for the evening or before getting into bed, take a couple of moments to examine your conscience. To do this, assume a prayerful position such as kneeling or lying prostrate, and invoke the Holy Spirit to help you examine your thoughts, words, and actions during the day. This does not need to be an exacting process. Ideally, first recount the blessings of the day and gives God thanks for them. Second, reflect upon and confess to God those of your actions, thoughts, and words that were not in conformity with God's holy will or are sinful. Third, after confessing your sins, make a heartfelt act of contrition, asking God for His mercy, forgiveness, and the grace necessary to avoid the near occasion of sin in the future. The Ten Commandments can be used as a guide by which you can examine your conscience, but sometimes these commandments may be too broad and general. Another powerful way to examine yourself is by using Christ's Beatitudes. For example:

**Blessed are the poor in Spirit** . . . Was I prideful, self-seeking, self-glorifying, self-important, placing myself above others today? Have I responded to the people and circumstances in my life with humility, accepting them as though they are from God?

**Blessed are the meek** . . . Did I allow anger to be the driving force behind my actions? Did I vent my anger, raise my voice, and act in a demeaning way to those around me? Do I allow Church politics, government politics, family situations, obstacles at work or at home to arouse my anger? Or do I give such situations to God and allow the Holy Spirit to help me deal with them rationally and calmly?

**Blessed are those who mourn** . . . Do I have true sorrow and contrition for my sins? Have I repented and done penance for my past sins? Do I seriously consider that my sins of the past may have led individuals to sin against God, perhaps even damnation? Do I ask God to make right my wrongs and redeem my omissions? Do I consider that it was for my sins that the Son of God was tortured and gave His life?

**Blessed are those who hunger and thirst for righteousness** . . . Do I desire the right over the wrong, the moral over the immoral? Do I rejoice when evil or immorality is lauded? Do I approve of videos, movies, posts, and tweets that contain illicit or immoral messages? Do I share such things, or find humor in them? Am I fair in my dealings with others, particularly in business and finances? Have I stolen anyone's goods, content, or good reputation? If so, have I made amends? Justice is seeking God first and giving Him His due: Do I seek God first in all matters? Do I give God the first fruits of my money and time?

**Blessed are the merciful** . . . Have I withheld forgiving someone who has offended me? Have I sought forgiveness from someone I have offended or sinned against? Have I judged, condemned, or criticized another unjustly? Have I judged another without considering my own wretchedness, failings, and sins?

**Blessed are the pure of heart** . . . Do I view the human body as an object of desire, to be used for my disordered gratification? Do I use pornography in any form? Do I avoid or do I submit to the temptation to click on ads, posts, or news feeds that display people in sexually provocative situations? Do I make every attempt to see a woman as an equal, with equal dignity, or do I reduce her to her bodily attributes? Do I use or manipulate people to obtain what I desire from them? Or do I love my neighbor for who they are, without expecting anything in return? Have I been jealous or envious of another's status, talents, gifts, or possessions? Do I praise God for His glory in others, even when I don't possess that particular glory?

+ JMJ +

**Blessed are those who suffer persecution for justice and Christ's sake** . . . Am I ashamed to share or display my belief in Jesus Christ? Am I afraid to pray in public? Do I avoid discussing my faith with others? Do I avoid or neglect protecting another's good actions, just cause, or beliefs in God because I am afraid of being persecuted?

## 4. Pray for Each Member of Your Family

As the priest of your family, it is your responsibility to present your wife and children, their intentions, needs, and spiritual and physical well-being to God daily. This indicates that you need to be aware of what is happening in their lives and know what their needs are. Your greatest petition for your wife and children, beyond worldly success, achievements, accomplishments, or acceptance by others, is their salvation and sanctification. Therefore, as the chief representative of your family, you are asking God to lavishly bless and grant favor to each member of your family.

## 5. Daily Morning Prayer
### (15 minutes/including 5 minutes of silence)

Secularists have been known to say, "Win the morning, win the day." The truth of this idea is born from the Christian ideal, particularly the monastic life, wherein the man who seeks God first is blessed in his work, efforts, and initiatives. Indeed, the Christian who gives God his morning's first moments will be given God's presence throughout his day. There exist many methods and forms of prayer that are far too numerous to mention here. The main purpose of your morning prayer is to allow yourself the time and space to cultivate a relationship with God and be drawn into His Trinitarian communion of Persons. Morning prayer is different than the morning offering: the morning offering is reporting for duty and asking God's blessing on one's day; the morning prayer is to be with and rest with God. Morning prayer consists of worship and praise, divine revelation as the source of conversation with God, and petition. To cultivate this divine conversation, a primer is very helpful, such as the Liturgy of the Hours, Sacred Scripture, or a reflection from a reliable devotional. The Liturgy of the Hours is an excellent resource that helps you "converse" with God by using preset psalms, prayers, and petitions that are segmented by the time, or "hours," of the day: Lauds is the morning prayer of the Church. Regardless of what source you use as the "launching pad" for your prayer with God, we must remember that these things are not "prayer" itself, but the "gas" that is poured on the hot coals of God's presence within the soul. The Holy Spirit then fans these embers into flame. After you have conversed with God, spend several minutes in silence, waiting upon Him. This time is essential to allowing God the time and space to speak or infuse Himself into your soul. After this period of silence, offer your petitions and thanksgiving to Him; and if possible, make a resolution that you will carry out throughout your day. End your prayer with a Glory Be.

\+ JMJ +

## 6. Daily Rosary

The Rosary is the chain that binds Satan. The Rosary is not a mere repetition of idle words, but a devotion to Our Blessed Mother, who leads us in meditation on Christ's life. Indeed, by "holding her hand," we see Jesus and His life through her eyes; and feeling with her heart, she helps to unlock the sacred mysteries of Christ's life, from His Incarnation through His Ascension, and the outpouring of His Holy Spirit on the Church. There exists a grave temptation or at least a tendency to rush through the prayers of the Rosary, rattling them off like an auctioneer; or to zone out and think of other things while saying the words. Due to the repetitive nature of the prayer, it is easy to understand how these things happen. To overcome such temptations, remember that the quality of prayer is more important than the quantity of words. The Rosary is a journey with Mary, following Christ and learning to be His disciple. Considering this, it can be highly beneficial to begin praying the Rosary by praying only one or two decades or by using a Scriptural Rosary. A Scriptural Rosary allows one to enter more deeply into the mystery being meditated upon by reciting a brief scriptural passage for each bead prior to praying the Hail Mary. For example, if you are praying the First Sorrowful Mystery, before saying the first Hail Mary, recite the verse: "Jesus took His disciples to the garden of Gethsemane and asked them to watch and pray." Prior to the second Hail Mary, you may recite the next verse: "Jesus said to His disciples, 'Pray that you may not fall into temptation.'" Prior to the third Hail Mary, "For the spirit is willing, but the flesh is weak," and so on. By praying the Rosary this way, you will be able to penetrate more deeply into the sacred mysteries of Christ, and thus His prayer can be more meaningful and profitable.

## 7. Evening Prayer

It has been said that how we finish our day is how we will finish our life. If we finish our day faithful in prayer and devotion, most likely we will complete our days devoted, faithful, and prayerful. The purpose of evening prayer is to offer worship to God and to cultivate conversation with God. As with morning prayer, to assist in fostering this conversation a primer such as the Liturgy of the Hours, Sacred Scripture, or a reflection from a reliable devotional is very helpful. As we've said, the Liturgy of the Hours helps you converse with God by using preset psalms, prayers, and petitions that are segmented by the time, or "hours," of the day. Vespers is the evening prayer of the Church. Prior to beginning evening prayer, spend a couple of moments in the presence of God, thanking Him for the blessings of the day and examining your conscience. After your examination of conscience, spend some time with God using Sacred Scripture, the Liturgy of the Hours, or a reflection. After you have conversed with God, spend several minutes in silence, waiting upon Him, again to allow God the time and space to speak or infuse Himself into your soul. An important note: we are often tempted to wind down by spending time on social media prior to sleep. Without realizing it, we are giving Satan a foothold in our spiritual life. After your evening prayer, avoid all social media and surrender your sleep to God.

## 8. One Daily Hidden Significant Sacrifice

It has been said that prayer without sacrifice is lip service, and sacrifice without prayer is a form of bodily training and self-mastery. Prayer inspires one to sacrifice; and sacrifice inspires the power of prayer. As priest of your domestic church, it is vital that you not only pray, but also sacrifice for your family's sanctity daily. If your sacrifice is to be efficacious, that is, able to transmit grace, it must have the character of secrecy, of being hidden. "Do not let your right hand know what your left hand is doing . . ." The Pharisees were said to blow a horn as they made a monetary donation, and Christ, speaking of them, said that they received their reward. Our sacrifice, therefore, is to be hidden; you are to perform the action without discussing or bringing attention to it; for by drawing attention to yourself, you have negated the power of the offering. A man who sacrifices does so in the image and in imitation of the Heavenly Father who "is in secret" (Mt 6:6). If our fatherhood is to reflect and relive the fatherhood of God, we are to carry out our sacrifices in a hidden way. Be not worried or concerned that you will not be rewarded. Glorify yourself and you will receive that reward. Glorify God and He cannot help but to glorify you; and this glory far surpasses any glory we can give ourselves. In addition to the sacrifice being secret, it ought to be significant; that is, your offering should cost you something. By setting aside that something you desire, are attached to, or have come to depend upon, and giving it to God as an offering, it becomes "holy," set apart, that God may use it to confer grace on you, your family, and humanity in the manner He sees fit. Suggested sacrifices that are significant to the average man are: sleeping on the floor; not using a pillow while you sleep; rising an hour early for prayer; committing to waking when the alarm rings without delay; taking a cold shower; skipping a meal(s); drinking nothing other than water; abstaining from alcohol; abstaining from sexual relations with your wife for a period of time; abstaining from the use of social media; donating money that you want to use for your own desires to a good cause; adoring the Blessed Sacrament several times a week, etc. The key is that the sacrifice be daily; that the motive is for God and the conversion of your family, Christian brothers, neighbors, and their families; that it is accomplished with the motivation of love and not necessarily "self-help" (for example: to lose weight); and that the sacrifice be hidden, as much as possible.

## 9. Reduce Forms of Media Such as Radio, Music, News, and Videos

To become capable of discerning the still, small, interior voice of God, it is vital that the voices of the world be muted. Without this first step, it will be gravely difficult to discern God's mission, vision, and plan for your life. A first step to becoming a man of silence who is capable of receiving God's impulses and divine inspirations is to silence the radio, music, news, and social media feeds while driving in the car or commuting. By doing so, your drive time can become prayer time—a very natural form of meditating—wherein you invite God into the areas of your life where you need divine guidance. Though at first it may feel awkward to be in silence, eventually your soul will crave such moments of solitude and eventually you will begin to notice that God is shaping your conscience and your motivations. Indeed, you will notice the effect of God's presence in your life.

+ JMJ +

## 10. Avoid Grumbling About or Demeaning Family Members

Complaining and grumbling about your children, your occupation, coworkers, friends, neighbors, finances, house, politics, the Church, and especially yourself, is a toxic poison that will not only make you appear weak, but will also place a massive burden on your wife. A good wife will often desire to fix things her husband struggles with, only to discover that she cannot. When this occurs, she begins to embody the stress, which can manifest itself in very negative ways, such as ill health, mental and psychological stress, depression and anxiety, or a lack of desire to thrive and live. As protector of your family, it is your duty to protect your wife first and foremost from *you*. To do this, every time you are tempted to complain, rather than doing so, find something encouraging and hopeful to focus on. If there is something problematic that needs to be discussed or resolved, commit yourself not to complain about the situation; but rather, consider ways that the it can be redeemed. Additionally, one of the most damaging things a man can do to himself and his marriage is to consistently speak negatively about himself. Your wife wants a leader, a lover, a spiritual warrior who is full of encouragement, hope, and confidence. If she senses that her husband has lost hope in himself, she may feel she is the reason for his personal sense of failure. In addition to this, she may even begin to look for the "confident warrior" in other men. "This is God's will for you: In all circumstances give thanks to God" (1 Thes 5:16). By being thankful to God for the good and the bad, the sufferings and the joys, you will become a man of confidence and joy; and such joy is contagious—especially in your marriage and family. Additionally, and perhaps more importantly, refrain from demeaning your wife in front of your children. Your show of disrespect to your wife will grant your children permission to disrespect their mother. Speaking critically of your wife or children has lasting, negative consequences that can take a lifetime to overcome. Words have a way of enduring in the person's heart long after they have been uttered.

## 11. Tithe Regularly/Give to the Poor

One the most effective ways that a child learns to be generous is witnessing his father giving generously to those in need. Sometimes, a dad will give his child the money to put in the collection basket at Mass, or have his child give money or food to a homeless person, in order to involve his child in this act of generosity. This almost always grants divine consolation and inculcates a love for the less fortunate. A generous father teaches his child that God the Father is generous. Indeed, if you as a human father help the poor, your child, who perhaps feels poor in spirit, will trust that God is generous and will provide. To be intentional in this area, keep extra cash on hand, so that if the occasion in which you are asked for help arises, you can provide. Archbishop Fulton Sheen, when asked, after giving money to beggars, why he did so when he knew they would probably misuse the money, responded, "Because I do not know which one is Jesus." A child will see Christ in his father who sees Christ in the poor.

+ JMJ +

## 12. Weekly/Biweekly Date with Your Wife

The greatest gift that a man, a father, can impart to his children is a united, harmonious, loving marriage with his wife. Security breeds security, love begets love. When children see the visible example of two people striving for union in God, they become secure, confident, and cannot help but want to experience and replicate such love. Too often, particularly as the family grows, life's responsibilities and obligations become complicated and overwhelming. Often, without noticing, years pass before a married couple realizes that they have grown distant from one another, and thus have grown cold in their love for one another. By making a weekly/biweekly date a priority, you will give your wife the opportunity to know that she is the most important person in your life, while also sending this message to your children. Your date does not need to be expensive, or a dinner out, but it can be that. The vital characteristics of a date are that you have private time that extends for a couple of hours; that your wife is listened to—not judged; that you look into her eyes and discover the woman you married and that she can feel this affection; and that you tell her she is beautiful and that you love her. A woman often forgets that she is beautiful because her husband has forgotten her beauty. To be affirmed in her beauty is one of her fundamental needs. By means of consistent dating, you will begin to see her beauty anew. Some couples will go out to a restaurant weekly, which can become costly; yet it can be the best money they will ever spend. Other couples have their date night at home, in a private area of the house away from the children, though this can be distracting. Regardless, the main point is that your date reminds her that she is a priority in your life, and she is loved. Another important point is that even if you and your wife are having a difficult time, or are in the midst of conflict, it is important, if possible, not to avoid the weekly/biweekly date. In fact, often by sitting across the table from one another, looking into one another, the disagreement diminishes or is resolved. Prudence is demanded, but if the couple is sincere in their desire for a better marriage, a date will help.

## 13. One Daily Intentional Act of Encouragement/Affection for Your Wife

St. John of the Cross said, "Where there is no love, put love, and there will be love." Often, a man can believe that because he is not "getting" what he wants from his marriage, that he has the right to distance himself from his wife. Yet, if you were to intentionally express your affection and encouragement to your wife daily, you would be putting love where perhaps there is no love, and eventually there will be love. Often, after birthing children, hormonal shifts, loss of muscle mass, a woman can gain weight, and over time the effects of age and time catch up. This is a cause to reaffirm her continually in her beauty and express that you delight in her—because she is fearful that you don't delight in her. Actions such as simply telling her that you are thankful she is your wife, or that she is beautiful; giving her a kiss and telling her you love her; mentioning that her new hair style looks good, or that you like the way she looks in what she is wearing; that she is a dedicated mother and wife, and without her your life would be miserable—these are a small sampling of ways to express your admiration and affection to her. A man may become embittered or resentful because his wife is not interested in sexual intercourse with him or has distanced herself from him in this area. If this resentment is not addressed, and if it takes hold of him, it may be only a matter of time before he falls prey to sexual sins and his marriage is undermined, if not destroyed. Though it may be counterintuitive, rather than shunning your wife because of her lack of attention to your sexual needs, you ought to reinvest yourself in her by means of acts of encouragement and affection—not for what you will get out of it, but for what you can put into it. If this is done in a self-giving manner, your wife more often than not may desire to give herself in return to you. Regardless, this is a sure path to becoming a saint: to love your wife and express it, especially when you don't "feel like it." Keep in mind Jesus Christ, who embraced the Cross for His bride—despite His flesh not "feeling like it."

## 14. Be Faithful to Your Wedding Vows

This needs no explanation. On the day of your wedding you vowed to be faithful to your wife until death. This commitment is a living figure and symbol of Christ's fidelity to His Church. Your mission is to be a living witness and expression of this faithful, undying love—no matter what comes. Lust in all its forms is the devil's weapon to separate love from sacrifice. Pornography is not the ultimate enemy. Satan is. He uses pornography as a weapon to bind the strong man and paralyze him from leading his family effectively. For how can he teach about and lead his family to Christ if he is bound by sin? He cannot. The devil's aim is to incapacitate you; and lust, pornography, and affairs are several of his methods to accomplish this. It is important to realize that the sins you commit are in a mysterious way transferred to your children. If lust and the use of pornography, or an adulterous relationship, have become an addictive pattern in your life, it is imperative that you go to confession weekly, if not twice a week; see a professional psychologist; develop friendships to hold you accountable in this area; and increase your prayer time. Faithfulness is the proof of love; and faithfulness demands sacrifice of our disordered attachments.

## 15. Pray with Your Wife Once a Day

Though a husband may pray with his wife during times of family prayer, it is important that he and his wife have a short, personal, prayer time, wherein they pray specifically for God to bless and heal their marriage and bless and sanctify their children. These private, personal prayer times between a couple unite the heart of the two into one and bless the marriage in unquantifiable ways. As protector of your domestic church, the enemy is more easily overcome by means of a harmonious, united marriage than by a father or mother who has their own individual faith.

## 16. Bless Your Wife Daily

As priest of your domestic church, God has entrusted you with the noble duty of conferring His blessing upon those in your care, which includes your wife. Though this may initially feel awkward, simply trace the cross over her forehead, and say, "May the Father, Son, and

+ JMJ +

Holy Spirit bless you now and forever." As you begin to feel more comfortable with this practice, you may add special intentions and ask God for particular graces and favors for your wife. This practice can concur after your private prayer time with your wife. Initially, this demands great courage to overcome the feeling of vulnerability and rejection. The feeling of awkwardness is an indication that the evil one hates this devotion and wants you to neglect your duty. Indeed, if you bless your wife, God will provide many graces that unify your marriage.

## 17. Ten Minutes of Daily Intentional Time with Your Wife

Family life is often busy, chaotic, and overwhelming. A mother can be swept away in the emotional and temporal demands of caring for her children. She needs time to share with her husband how she is interpreting her children's welfare and her own motherhood, along with her personal existence as a human being. In other words, she needs time to share her heart. Communication leads to communion. If a husband wants true, authentic, deep communion with his wife, he will need to set aside a little time each day to hear his wife's heart. This daily communication leads to the couple being comfortable with expressing their personal needs to one another. This ability to feel secure and safe in expressing needs is essential to a healthy marriage. It is important to always bear in mind that no spouse can fulfill their spouse's needs—only Christ can. Yet, what makes a spouse feel, experience, and know that he or she is loved is when the spouse intentionally attempts to address the other's need.

However, a husband cannot address his wife's needs if she is not communicating them to him, and vice versa. For this reason, ten minutes of daily intentional time with your wife will help the two of you become expert communicators and experience true communion in Christ.

## 18. Biweekly Son Man-Date/Daughter-Date

Children crave individual attention from their parents and in particular from their father. In times past, families and family life were more agrarian, and therefore the family, by its very nature, demanded that children spend more time with their fathers. In the modern age, due to technological advances, particularly in the realm of travel, children receive less individual time and attention from their fathers. By establishing a biweekly man-date with your son or daughter-date with your daughter, you reestablish a connection between you and your child. This commitment to your child communicates that he or she is important to you—important enough for you to sacrifice your own agendas and initiatives for them. The dates need not be anything elaborate; simply going out for breakfast or coffee is good. The main objective of this time spent with your child is to solidify your relationship. Listen and let the child know you care and have an interest in his or her life; express God the Father's generosity (through food and time) and love (attention and listening). Don't have an agenda—meaning, don't take your child out and then drop a bomb about how you are disappointed in them, or have a problem with them that needs resolving. If this occurs, your child will not trust you or want to spend time with you. This demands that the date is a safe zone in which no discipline occurs, and no harsh criticism is made. One key to making this effective is selecting a consistent day and time when the date will occur. If you choose every other Friday, make this a priority, and don't break your promise. If a father consistently breaks the "promise" of the daughter-date or man-date, he will break his child's heart. Your greatest treasures are your wife and children. The best money and time you will ever spend is on them.

## 19. One Daily Intentional Act of Encouragement or Affection for Your Child

A child in today's culture is continually measuring himself against the world's impossible standards. Peer culture and persuasive and pervasive media messages can convince a child to find value and worth in the world, and in the world's evaluation of them. If and when this happens, a child's value will shift based on how they are received by their peers. It is vital that your child knows and understands that their worth and personal value does not shift based on whether he's accepted by his peers. To offset and overcome this mentality, it is vital that your child knows that he or she is chosen and not just accepted. To be accepted means that the child is welcome to live with you, use your house and possessions, etc. To let them feel chosen is to intentionally reach out to the child with a hug, a kiss, a blessing, a word of encouragement, or to sit down next to them in order to converse. The more a child senses that they are valued because of who they are, the more they will believe in God, who loves them for who they are. You can help provide your child with this sense of value by telling her that you are proud of her; that you love him; that you noticed that he did X, Y, Z and commend him for it. A father's words have prophetic power: speak hope and personal value into them and they will become people of hope who understand their God-given value. Yet, this is a two-edged sword: if you bite at, demean, discourage, and criticize your child, it will no doubt have negative consequences on his ability to perceive himself as a gift from God. Action steps that can help you in affirming and encouraging your child include identifying things about your child that are of God, and from God; verbally acknowledging those gifts, talents, and abilities; intentionally telling your child that you love him or her; and being physically affectionate with hugs and kisses, roughhousing, etc.

## 20. Install Internet Filtration Software

No longer does one need to look for immoral, illicit, pornographic content. No. It is looking for us . . . and our children. Even websites and apps that appear to be safe and secure can often be compromised by links and ads that eventually lead to an immoral trap. The porn industry has spent an enormous amount of money and time devising strategies to have children encounter pornography at an early age, for the purpose of engendering a life-long addiction. This addiction means financial growth and stability for those who produce pornography. It has been said that fifteen seconds on the internet can destroy fifteen years of parenting. As protector of your family, it is important to avoid the all-too-common belief: "Not my child." We must understand that it is not your child who is evil, warped, and perverted; but it is your child who can become a victim of such evils. Considering this, it is important to research and determine which internet filtration software is most effective and then purchase and install it.

## 21. Bless Your Child Daily

You as the human father are a link between heaven and earth, between God and your child. You are called to be the face of the Father that your child cannot see; the voice of the Father that your child cannot hear; and the touch of the Father that your child cannot feel. In the moment of blessing your child, you become the face, the voice, and the touch of the heavenly Father to your child. The fatherly blessing is very powerful, and inculcates a deep love, respect, and trust in your children—trust in you and your fatherhood, and trust in God and His Fatherhood. As with blessing your wife, initially you will experience a feeling of awkwardness and vulnerability, but over time this practice becomes a very loving and natural way to express your love for your child. The keys to blessing your child are selecting a consistent time (for many fathers this is prior to bedtime); tracing the sign of the cross over your child's forehead; invoking God's favor and blessing upon your child, and the grace of restful sleep (if it is prior to bedtime). Hug and embrace your child after the blessing. It may be beneficial to develop your own personal blessing. Regardless, consistency and calling down God the Father's blessing in Christ Jesus' name, and your face, voice, and touch, are the key components of this grace-filled practice.

## 22. Nightly Family Dinner

There appears to be a direct correlation between the massive decrease in families eating dinner together and the decline in Mass attendance. The family dinner reflects Holy Mass. As father of your family, you are like the Heavenly Father, who gathers his family around the "altar"—that is, your dinner table. Prior to dinner, together offer Him thanksgiving from your heart for the good that God has given. As priest of your family, you not only lead your family in this ode of gratitude, but also instill this virtue of thanksgiving in each of your family members. Family dinner is a safe zone. This is not the place to discipline your children for not completing their chores, or for failing Math. Family dinner is a time in which you can help foster joyful, encouraging conversation about important topics by asking each family member: How was your day? What made it good/bad? Tell me a little more about this ... It is good to tell stories from your past or recent experiences that relate to a topic, making your time enjoyable but also educational. As a father, you are to help your children understand and interpret the world and current events in light of the Gospel. The main point is that your family becomes bonded to God through your gratitude, and also bonded to you through healthy conversations. You are an icon of God the Father. If you express interest in each of your family member's lives, they will more likely believe that they are interesting and worthy of interest, and that God is interested in them. One major obstacle to family dinner in the modern age is the overwhelming amount of extracurricular activities and commitments. Evaluate whether these activities are at the service of your family or whether your family is at the service of these activities. Determine which ones are a priority and sacrifice the others. Often, we sacrifice the family for the sake of activities, rather than sacrificing activities for the sake of God and the family. If nightly family dinner is impossible, make every effort to identify at least three nights a week that your family will meet for dinner. Good food, good conversation, prayer with thanksgiving, and an interested father's heart are the key elements of your family dinner.

## 23. Sacred Images

Mindfulness of responsibilities and the commitment to duty often can be a cause for inadvertently forgetting about God, His Son, Jesus, and the saints who are cheering us on to victory. God is a family, a Trinity of Persons, and has created the human race to be an eternal part of this family. The saints are those who are fully embraced as family members of God's house. We hang photos of family members to remind us of them. How much more do we benefit by having sacred images of Jesus Christ, the Sacred Heart, a crucifix, the Blessed Mother, St. Joseph, saints, or a scene from the Gospel hanging on the walls of our home? These sacred images offer us a continual reminder to call upon our family in heaven to aid us as we travail this valley of tears. Additionally, these images leave an imprint of the divine upon our children's souls, reminding them to raise their hearts and minds to those things above and not the things below.

## 24. Sunday Gospel Reflection

The Word of God is powerful, capable of discerning thoughts and transforming the human heart. Often, when we hear the Gospel on Sunday, we overlook or miss powerful lessons contained in the Word. Even though a priest gives a homily that expounds on the Gospel, the message may not resonate in our children's hearts. A way to prepare our children to receive more from the Gospel is by selecting a weeknight to read the upcoming Sunday's Gospel during family prayer time and discuss it. Themes and ideas that arise from your discussion will help your child to understand the Gospel more clearly, so that at Mass, your child will benefit more from the proclamation of the Word. Some ways to make Sunday Gospel reflection beneficial are: 1) Select a particular night of the week to have your Sunday Gospel reflection and keep it consistent. 2) Read it ahead of time and consider what you think the Lord may be communicating to you. 3) Have one of your family members read the Gospel. 4) After the reading the Gospel, say together, "Praise to you Lord Jesus Christ." 5) Then ask your family if anyone has any thoughts, comments, or questions. Keep in mind that these are their personal reflections. Considering this, try not to say things like, "No. That is not what the Gospel is saying." Or, "Do you really believe that?" The key is to invite discussion and allow the Lord to lead your family to truthful, inspiring conclusions. Sometimes a child will offer a challenging question or comment. This is good in that it can inspire a healthy search for God and His truth. After everyone has commented, you can add your thoughts, and perhaps suggest a call to action. For example: "Let's make a commitment to pray for the dead." Or, "Let's strive to go out of our way to do

+ JMJ +

kind acts for one another." 6) Each person can then offer their own prayer intentions. 7) End with thanksgiving to God for His Word and pray a Glory Be.

## 25. Family Prayer Time

The family who prays together stays together (Fr. Patrick Peyton). And even more importantly, a family that prays together stays with God. The key to raising a holy family is being committed to daily family prayer time. Many of your personal methods of praying can be used during family prayer time. For example, the family can pray a couple of decades of a Scriptural Rosary, Sunday Gospel reflection, Vespers (evening prayer) from the Liturgy of Hours, reading of Scripture, etc. The secret to family prayer is simply doing it. As the father, you have incredible influence on your family. If you lead, most of the time your family will follow. Lead your family to Jesus and Jesus will lead your family. Action steps for implementing and maintaining family prayer include: 1) Establishing a time each evening for family prayer time. 2) Don't make it long—this can make family prayer time drudgery, especially if the children sense that they are not able to complete homework or have free time. 3) Be consistent, press on, and don't give up. 4) Don't be a drill sergeant and criticize your children for their posture or their lack of attentiveness. 5) Make your prayer personal. Teach your children to pray from their heart. One way to accomplish this is to ask them to voice their petitions. Whether you use the Liturgy of the Hours, Sacred Scripture, or a reflection from a devotional, end your family prayer time with personal prayers of thanksgiving, petition, and praise.

## 26. Family Evening Time

If a modern man was to calculate, at the end of his life, the amount of hours spent at work and then compare them to the amount of hours spent with his family, he would discover that he spent nearly two thirds of his waking hours working and approximately less than a sixth of his waking hours with his family. Considering this, and the fact that we only have, on average, eighteen years of a child living at home with us, our time spent with our children is fleeting and precious. One way to reclaim time with our family for the purpose of fostering strong relationships with them is by making the hours between dinner and bedtime exclusively dedicated to the family. To do this effectively, strive to shut off the television and social media; shut off mobile devices, including your phone, unless you need to be on call; and identify activities for the whole family. After dinner is done and the dishes and kitchen have been cleaned, and after subtracting family prayer time, there is a small chunk of time to spend with your family. This time together is a great tool for solidifying your family and protecting them from the enemy. Too often, children will venture off to their own rooms with their own personal mobile devices and be swept away in virtual worlds that distance them from God and the Church. Your time together as a family is a great aid in overcoming this divisional tactic.

## 27. One Holy Hour a Week

Once per week, make a visit to a chapel that has perpetual Eucharistic Adoration. Make it a point to find a local parish and spend time

+ JMJ +

before our Lord's Eucharistic Presence in the tabernacle. Unfortunately, in modern times, Catholic churches are locked, and for good reasons. Yet we must make every effort to either contact the pastor of a parish, obtain a key, or request entrance to the church for a time of prayer. There is nearly nothing as life-changing and transforming as spending time with Christ in Adoration. You cannot give what you do not possess. To give God you must have God; and to have God you must spend time with God; and one of the most powerful ways to spend time with God is in Eucharistic Adoration. By adoring the Lord in His littleness, silence, and hiddenness, you will be given the power to rejoice and be effective in the little, silent, hidden character of your fatherhood. God cannot be outdone in His generosity. Ultimately, it would be ideal to visit our Lord in the Most Blessed Sacrament daily. Regardless, by giving an hour to our Lord once per week, He will grant you incalculable blessings.

## 28. Frequent Sacraments: Take Child to One Daily Mass a Week/Monthly Confession

One way to convince your child to go to a daily morning Mass is to go out for breakfast or coffee afterward. This connects the two experiences of Mass and Dad time. As the child ages, they will associate Holy Mass with a feeling of goodness, warmth, and love, because of the time you spent with them. This connects your love as a father with the love of the heavenly Father. Daily Mass also allows your child to have a more personal connection with the Mass and with Jesus in the Eucharist. Often, Sunday Mass can be distracting and overwhelming. Daily Mass, with its character of silence, affords a more personal experience of Christ, His Word, and His Most Holy Sacrament. Additionally, take your child and yourself to the Sacrament of Confession at least once a month. A father who admits that he is a sinner and seeks God's forgiveness sets the standard for his child.

## 29. Establish Your Tent of Meeting

Sometimes we need to "go there," to a place of pilgrimage, to find God "in here," in our hearts. God commanded Moses to erect a "tent of meeting" outside the camp, where Israelites could go to meet with God and receive His guidance. Often, we wonder why our prayer time is compromised, distracted, or ineffective. One of the reasons is that we are praying in an environment that is anything but prayerful. When we look around during prayer, we often see paperwork that needs completion, projects that need finishing, dishes that need washing, garbage that needs taking out. The mess of life tends to creep in, making a mess in our soul. A way to battle against, even overcome this disadvantage is to allocate and dedicate a place in your home to be reserved exclusively for prayer. This could be a closet, a basement, or a spare bedroom. Regardless, identify that space and then claim it for the Lord by hanging sacred images there. Use a table as an altar and set your Bible on it; use candles and incense; place statues of Our Lord, our Blessed Mother, and St. Joseph as reminders of your heavenly family. By dedicating a space in your home exclusively to God, you can more effectively dedicate yourself exclusively to God. Additionally, your family will come to understand that God is not an afterthought but the primary reason for your existence.

+ JMJ +

## 30. Celebrate Feast Days/Abide Fast Days

A good father connects his domestic church with the liturgical calendar of Holy Mother Church. Therefore, on days of fasting, he guides his family to fast and pray in a way that honors the Lord, without grumbling or complaining. On solemnities and special feast days, especially those related to our Lord Jesus, His Blessed Mother, St. Joseph, and holy patron saints—after whom our children are named—we should strive to be festive, with feasting, desserts, music, hymn singing, and to celebrate with family and friends. Another good practice is to honor St. Joseph every Wednesday. By doing so, we create a true liturgical Catholic culture in our domestic church, and our families become connected with the life of Christ as expressed by His Church. One way to make patron saints' feasts more meaningful is to take the child out on a special date. Birthdays and/or baptism days of individual members of the family should also be highly festive and celebrated. Rather than religion being understood as an imposition and a burden, by celebrating such special days we emphasize the joy and generosity of God, and such joy is winsome.

## 31. Abstain from All Work on Sunday

The third commandment is not "Do not work on Sunday," but rather to "Keep holy the Sabbath (the Lord's Day)." Too often, we use Sunday as the day of the week to catch up with duties and chores, or to get ahead by working overtime. Yet God calls us to make Sunday holy by setting it aside for him. The Day of the Lord should be celebratory, familial, and should express to God gratitude and joy for His presence and for the gifts in our lives. We ought to sacrifice our own personal pursuits on Sunday for the Lord who sacrificed Himself for us. Ways to make the Lord's Day a day of holiness include: going to Mass on Sunday; having a big breakfast with the family afterward; inviting friends and family over for Sunday dinner; doing something fun as a family; and turning off the television, streaming content, and social media. Don't go shopping or out to restaurants. And offer prayers of thanksgiving before dinner with family and friends. Our culture has made Sunday another day of labor, or a way to increase the value of your home. Reclaim it for the Lord and for your family by setting it aside for God, and God will not be outdone in generosity.

## 32. Initiate and Be involved in Family Work

Whether it is doing the dishes after dinner, Saturday housecleaning, landscaping or building retaining walls, remodeling the house, doing plumbing or electrical work, mowing the lawn, sweeping the floor, or changing the little one's diapers, the father should set the pace of self-giving love, that is, initiate an act of service for his family. This simply means that he alerts everyone to the task and then works alongside his children in carrying out the chore at hand. With joy and a mind for excellence, he encourages his children to do everything with excellence—not for a wage, but rather in the service of the family. The family is to be like the Trinity: three self-giving persons who are one. We only discover ourselves by giving ourselves away. Familial work is a tremendous gift in that it teaches parents and children to be gifts to one another for the greater good; and in doing this work, everyone discovers personal potential and the joy of serving others. By being involved in familial work, your children come to respect you. Too often a father will leave household chores to his wife and children and venture off to his own hobbies. This type of leadership inculcates disdain and resentment not only for the work, but also for the father. Jesus and Joseph crafted the cross of self-donation in the workshop in Nazareth. Let us, as fathers, learn from them.

## 33. Sanctify Your Work

"In whatever you do, do it from the heart, as to the Lord, not to men" (Col 3:23). Work is a substantial part of a man's life. Not only does he spend much of his life laboring for a wage, but work is an outlet for creativity and charity, in which man can discover meaning and experience personal fulfillment. Work can also be a massive burden and extremely dissatisfying. Whether work is fulfilling or dissatisfying, it can be redeemed by God, by offering it to Christ in union with His salvific work. A father can make his work meaningful, ultimately, by first doing his best to labor with excellence as though he is working for God. Second, he is to offer his work for the redemption of his wife and children, asking God to lavishly grant graces to his family. Yet a father must always bear in mind that his occupation is in the service of his vocation. Therefore his work should not eclipse the primary duties of his vocation, such as family prayer, his own prayer life, family dinner, and the like. There may be circumstances regarding his work that are beyond a father's control, and yet he should do all that he can to place work at the service of his family, rather than his family at the service of his work.

+ JMJ +

## Notes

i   "He shall not contend, nor cry out, neither shall any man hear his voice in the streets" (Mt 12:19); "He shall not cry, nor have respect to person, neither shall his voice be heard abroad" (Is 42:2).

ii   The Lord Jesus, speaking about the glory and respect that men afford said, "I receive glory not from men" (Jn 5:41); and after the miracle of the multiplication of the loaves and fishes, the people wanted to make Jesus king, but he hid in the mountains: "Jesus therefore, when he knew that they would come to take him by force, and make him king, fled again into the mountain himself alone" (Jn 6:15). Indeed, "It is good to confide in the Lord, rather than to have confidence in man" (Ps 118:8). The true Christian man strives to overcome the temptation to win favor and respect of men, rather than looking to God for his true value. "Blessed is the servant who esteems himself no better when he is praised and exalted by people than when he is considered worthless, simple and despicable, for what man is before God, that he is and nothing more" (St. Francis of Assisi).

iii   As mentioned in the preface, there are some who contend that St. Joseph was not a true father because he was not the biological father of Jesus; or at the very least he was a foster father. However, many saints and doctors of the Church, including the Blessed Virgin herself, refer to St. Joseph as a father of Jesus. St. Joseph is traditionally called "foster father'" of Jesus, or Jesus' adopted father. However, St. Joseph's fatherhood is more than adoptive. According to St. Augustine, "Joseph is not to be denied as father of Christ under pretext that he had not generated Him, for Joseph would rightly be father even of a son who he had not generated from his wife, if he had adopted him from outside [his marriage]." "Luke did not call Mary Christ's sole parent; he had no hesitation in calling both His parents . . . When, then, he records that Christ was born not of the act of Joseph but of Mary the Virgin, on what grounds does he call Joseph father unless we correctly understand that this was by the very bond of marriage." And again, "Was it not for another reason, namely, that Joseph was the father of Christ, who had been born of his wife—father so much more intimately than if He had been adopted from outside the marriage?" "Joseph's relationship to Jesus thus becomes something that far surpasses adoptive fatherhood. (Francis L. Filas, S.J., *Joseph and Jesus: A Theological Study of Their Relationship*, p. 44).

iv   There are some who contend that our Lord was not "reared" or "raised" by St. Joseph, for He was God the Son. We must remember that the Son, the Second Person of the Trinity, is one divine Person with two natures, divine and human. Jesus' human nature encountered and experienced his surroundings anew, and therefore, humanly speaking, allowed himself to be introduced to these realities by His parents. It is important that we make a distinction between Divine need and Divine Will. When we speak about man and his participation in God's plan from the context of Divine need, we can only conclude that God needs no one to complete Him. Therefore, we cannot assert that any human being, even the Most Blessed Virgin Mary is needed from the divine perspective. However, God by His Divine Will allows Himself to become subject to the authority of man for the purpose of teaching us that subjection to the Divine Will, which demands a true self-emptying and personal abandonment to God, is essential to the spiritual life. Therefore, God willed that the Word made flesh obey His human parents, that He is assisted by Simon of Cyrene, and taught by St. Joseph, not because He needed any of them, but rather because He willed it to give us an example. Our Lord Jesus did not need to be baptized by the holy Sprit for He was already united fully to the Holy Spirit. Yet, Jesus allows John to baptize Him. Our Lord, as Head, not only obtains for His Body the Holy Spirit, but also demonstrates the necessity that we submit to others who administer the Sacraments. This dynamic applies to Jesus' relationship to St. Joseph: Joseph was called to name the Son, though He already had been named. Joseph was called to teach the Child though He already had perfect knowledge. Joseph was called to raise the child though he was already exalted and complete. Joseph blessed the one who was benediction Himself. Why? Jesus' submission to St. Joseph as teacher, father, leader, as in His baptism by John, teaches us: 1) submission to the Divine Will is essential in all matters; and 2) as the Head of the Body—Christ—does, so must we also follow; and 3) that there exists a proper hierarchal order in the family.

"It is no exaggeration to think that it was precisely from his 'father' Joseph that Jesus learned—at the human level—that steadfast interiority which is a presupposition of authentic justice" (Pope Benedict XVI). And again, "The growth of Jesus 'in wisdom and in stature, and in favor with God and man' (Lk 2:52) took place within the Holy Family under the eyes of Joseph, who had the important task of 'raising' Jesus, that is, feeding, clothing and educating him in the Law in a trade, in keeping with the duties of a father" (*Redemptoris Custos*, John Paul II). And again, "The very purpose of the virginal union as determined by God was that it should prepare for our Lord's coming, should receive Him in its midst, and should rear Him to adult manhood" (Filas, *Joseph and Jesus*, p. 156).

v   The fist chapter of St. Matthew's Gospel lists the Lord Jesus' genealogy, which demonstrates that the Davidic blood line culminated in Jesus and was conferred upon him by St. Joseph. Hence the title "Son of David."

vi   "And they put over his head his accusation written: THIS IS JESUS THE KING OF THE JEWS" (Mt 27:37).

vii   By means of baptism the Christian participates in the Kingship of Christ. "Christ, high priest and unique mediator, has made of the Church 'a kingdom, priests for his God and Father.' The whole community of believers is, as such, priestly. The faithful exercise their baptismal priesthood through their participation, each according to his own vocation, in Christ's mission as priest, prophet, and king. Through the sacraments of Baptism and Confirmation the faithful are "consecrated to be . . . a holy priesthood" (CCC 1546).

viii   2 Cor 4:4: "god of this world."

ix   1 Cor 3:16: " Know you not, that you are the temple of God, and that the Spirit of God dwelleth in you?"

x   St. Albert the Great is clear that Jesus was conceived within St. Joseph's marriage: "The Gospel does not say that he was conceived before the marriage pact. it implies that conception occurred later, when it states, 'When she had been betrothed.' Whatever happens after the marriage agreement, which is there called a betrothal, pertains in its entirety to marriage" (Filas, *Joseph and Jesus*, p. 67). CCC 956: the intercession of the saints.

xi   Eph 5:25: "Husbands, love your wives, as Christ also loved the church, and delivered himself up for it."

xii   Simeon prophesied to Mary: "And thy own soul a sword shall pierce, that, our of

+ JMJ +

many hearts, thoughts may be revealed" (Lk 2:35). The physical sword that pierced Jesus' side also spiritually and mystically pierced Mary's heart. At the beginning of His life, Mary held in her arms the naked body of the Christ Child; at the end of His life she held the naked body of the God-man who had been crucified. Mary's joys had become her sorrows. The devotion of the Stations of the Cross place the words of Naomi on Mary's lips: "Call me not Noemi (that is beautiful), but call me Mara (that is bitter), for the Almighty hath quite filled me with bitterness" (Ruth 1:20).

xiii    According to George Foot Moore, "Betrothal was a formal act by which the woman became legally the man's wife; unfaithfulness on her part was adultery and punishable as such; if the relation was dissolved a bill of divorce was required. Some time elapsed after the bridegroom claimed the fulfillment of the agreement before the bride was taken to her husband's house and the marriage consummated. The term employed for betrothal, *kiddushin*, has religious associations; it is an act by which the woman is, so to speak, consecrated to her husband, set apart for him exclusively" (Filas, *Joseph and Jesus*, p. 17).

xiv    Mt 1:18: "When as his mother Mary was espoused to Joseph, before they came together, she was found with child, of the Holy Spirit."

xv    "If any man commit adultery with the wife of another, and defile his neighbor's wife: let them be put to death, both the adulterer and the adulteress" (Lev 20:10); "The priest therefore shall offer it, and set it before the Lord. And he shall take holy water in an earthen vessel, and he shall cast a little earth of the pavement of the tabernacle into it. And when the woman shall stand before the Lord, he shall uncover her head, and shall put on her hands the sacrifice of remembrance, and the oblation of jealousy: and he himself shall hold the most bitter waters, whereon he hath heaped curses with execration. And he shall adjure her, and shall say: If another man hath not slept with thee, and if thou be not defiled by forsaking thy husband's bed, these most bitter waters, on which I have heaped curses, shall not hurt thee. But if thou hast gone aside from thy husband, and art defiled, and hast lain with another man: These curses shall light upon thee: The Lord make thee a curse, and an example for all among his people: may he make thy thigh to rot, and may thy belly swell and burst asunder. Let the cursed waters enter into thy belly, and may thy womb swell and thy thigh rot. And the woman shall answer, Amen, amen. And the priest shall write these curses in a book, and shall wash them out with the most bitter waters, upon which he hath heaped the curses, And he shall give them her to drink. And when she hath drunk them up, The priest shall take from her hand the sacrifice of jealousy, and shall elevate it before the Lord, and shall put it upon the altar: yet so as first, To take a handful of the sacrifice of that which is offered, and burn it upon the altar: and so give the most bitter waters to the woman to drink. And when she hath drunk them, if she be defiled, and having despised her husband be guilty of adultery, the malediction shall go through her, and her belly swelling, her thigh shall rot: and the woman shall be a curse, and an example to all the people" (Num 5:16-27); "And said to him: Master, this woman was even now taken in adultery. Now Moses in the law commanded us to stone such a one. But what sayest thou?" (Jn 8:4–5).

xvi    Psalm 1 speaks of the "just" who "know the way of the Lord" (1:6), as opposed to the wicked who will perish. It is the just man whose "will is in the law of the Lord, and on his law he shall meditate day and night" (Ps 1:2).

xvii    "But according to Jerome and Origen, (Joseph) had no suspicion of adultery.

For Joseph knew Mary's chastity; he had read the Scriptures that a virgin will conceive" (Isa 7:14), and "there will come forth a rod out of the root of Jesse, and a flower will rise up out of his root" (Isa 11:1); he also knew that Mary was descended from David. Hence, he more easily believed that this had been fulfilled in her than that she had fornicated" (St. Thomas Aquinas, *Commentary on the Gospel of St. Matthew*, 117).

xviii    Mt 6:33: "Seek ye therefore first the kingdom of God, and his justice, and all these things shall be added unto you."

xix    See Genesis 2:15: "And the Lord God took man, and put him into the paradise for pleasure, to dress it, and keep it." Adam was given the task to dress and keep the garden. The Hebrew word for dress, *abad*, means "to cherish"; and the Hebrew word for keep, *shamar*, means "to protect." Adam was also warned that if he was to eat the forbidden fruit from the tree of knowledge of good and evil, he would die. "But of the tree of knowledge of good and evil, thou shalt not eat. For in what day soever thou shalt eat of it, thou shalt die the death" (Gen 2:17). From these observations we can conclude that Adam was aware that his duty was to protect the garden, and his wife, from death.

xx    Gen 3:6: "And the woman saw that the tree was good to eat, and fair to the eyes, and delightful to behold: and she took of the fruit thereof, and did eat, and gave to her husband who did eat."

xxi    Ibid.

xxii    CCC 398: "In that sin man *preferred* himself to God and by that very act scorned him. He chose himself over and against God, against the requirements of his creaturely status and therefore against his own good. Constituted in a state of holiness, man was destined to be fully "divinized" by God in glory. Seduced by the devil, he wanted to "be like God", but "without God, before God, and not in accordance with God.""

xxiii    St. Paul connects the original Adam with the New Adam, Jesus Christ. See 1 Cor 15:45: "The first man Adam was made into a living soul; the last Adam into a quickening spirit"; and also, "Wherefore as by one man sin entered into this world and by sin death: and so death passed upon all men, in whom all have sinned. For until the law sin was in the world: but sin was not imputed, when the law was not. But death reigned from Adam unto Moses, even over them also who have not sinned, after the similitude of the transgression of Adam, who is a figure of him who was to come. But not as the offence, so also the gift. For if by the offence of one, many died: much more the grace of God and the gift, by the grace of one man, Jesus Christ, hath abounded unto many. And not as it was by one sin, so also is the gift. For judgment indeed was by one unto condemnation: but grace is of many offences unto justification. For if by one man's offence death reigned through one; much more they who receive abundance of grace and of the gift and of justice shall reign in life through one, Jesus Christ. Therefore, as by the offence of one, unto all men to condemnation: so also, by the justice of one, unto all men to justification of life. For as by the disobedience of one man, many were made sinners: so also, by the obedience of one, many shall be made just. Now the law entered in that sin might abound. And where sin abounded, grace did more abound. That as sin hath reigned to death: so also, grace might reign by justice unto life everlasting, through Jesus Christ our Lord" (Rom 5:12-21).

xxiv    "Why did Joseph want to leave his spouse, Mary? Listen not to my opinion, but to that of the Fathers. He thought to leave Her for the same reason why Peter kept the Lord at a distance, saying, 'Depart from me, Lord, for I am a sinner' (Lk 5:8), or the Centurion did

+ JMJ +

not want the Lord to come to his house, saying: 'Lord, I am not worthy that you enter my house' (Mt 8:8). Likewise, Joseph, retaining himself to be unworthy and sinful, went away saying that he would not be able to live with a woman who was so great, whose wonderful and superior dignity he feared. He saw and feared the woman who bore a certain sign of the divine presence; and since he was not able to penetrate the meaning of this mystery, he wanted to leave Her in a hidden way. Peter was fearful in the face of such power, the Centurion before the majesty of His presence. Also, Joseph, as a man, feared the newness of such a great miracle; he was afraid of the profoundness of such mystery; and decided to leave Her in a hidden way" (St. Bernard, *Laudes Mariae* 2, 13–16)

xxv "And therefore, considering himself unworthy to live with such great sanctity, he wished to hide her away, just as Peter said, depart form me, for I am sinful man, O Lord (Luke 5:8). Hence, he did not wish to hand her over, i.e., to take her to himself, and receive her in marriage, considering himself unworthy" (St. Thomas Aquinas, *Commentary on the Gospel of St. Matthew*, 117).

xxvi Eph 4:1.

xxvii Mt 1:20.

xxviii Psalm 16:7.

xxix St. Joseph's act of pondering over his personal dilemma was not mere casual consideration, but rather was an intense, spirit-rending event in which his soul was deeply grieved by the potential loss of Mary—as indicated by the Greek word used for "while he thought," *enthyméomai,* which can be translated as a "state of condition, passionate frame of mind, moved by strong provoking impulses." From this we can conclude that Joseph was praying about his sore dilemma.

xxx See Lk 1:28.

xxxi See Jn 1:14.

xxxii "The family finds in the plan of God the Creator and Redeemer not only its identity, what it is, but also its mission, what it can and should do. The role that God calls the family to perform in history derives from what the family is; its role represents the dynamic and existential development of what it is. Each family finds within itself a summons that cannot be ignored, and that specifies both its dignity and its responsibility: family, become what you are. Accordingly, the family must go back to the 'beginning' of God's creative act if it is to attain self-knowledge and self-realization in accordance with the inner truth not only of what it is but also of what it does in history. And since in God's plan it has been established as an 'intimate community of life and love'" (*Redemptoris Custos* 48). "The family has the mission to become more and more what it is, that is to say, a community of life and love, in an effort that will find fulfillment, as will everything created and redeemed, in the Kingdom of God. Looking at it in such a way as to reach its very roots, we must say that the essence and role of the family are in the final analysis specified by love. Hence the family has the mission to guard, reveal and communicate love, and this is a living reflection of and a real sharing in God's love for humanity and the love of Christ the Lord for the Church His bride." (*Familiaris Consortio* 17, November 22, 1981, John Paul II). And "God became a man and a member of a specific family so that all men and women might be able to become members of the supernaturally-constituted family of God, the Church. This means that each Christian family is a reflection of an eternal mystery, for it is "a communion of persons, a sign and image of the communion of the Father and the Son in the Holy Spirit" (CCC, 2205).

xxxiii "God himself is an eternal exchange of love, Father, Son and Holy Spirit, and he has destined us to share in that exchange" (CCC 221).

xxxiv "The first witnesses of Christ's birth, the shepherds, found themselves not only before the Infant Jesus but also a small family: mother, father and newborn son. God had chosen to reveal himself by being born into a human family and the human family thus became an icon of God! God is the Trinity, he is a communion of love; so is the family despite all the differences that exist between the Mystery of God and his human creature, an expression that reflects the unfathomable Mystery of God as Love. In marriage the man and the woman, created in God's image, become "'one flesh' (Gen 2: 24), that is a communion of love that generates new life. The human family, in a certain sense, is an icon of the Trinity because of its interpersonal love and the fruitfulness of this love." (Pope Benedict XVI, Feast of the Holy Family, St. Peter's Square, Sunday, December 27, 2009).

xxxv "The Christian family is a communion of persons, a sign and image of the communion of the Father and the Son in the Holy Spirit" (CCC 2205). *And again*, "When they become parents, spouses receive from God the gift of a new responsibility. Their parental love is called to become for the children the visible sign of the very love of God, 'from whom every family in heaven and on earth is named'" (*Familiaris Consortio*, November 22, 1981, John Paul II).

xxxvi The Holy Family is the archetype and model of the human reflection of the Trinity. This family is the example for all families of what they are called to reflect and reveal. According to St. Francis de Sales, "There is, then, no doubt that St. Joseph was endowed with all the graces and all the gifts that were required for the care which the Eternal Father willed to give him of the temporal and domestic economy of our Lord, and of the guidance of His family. This was composed of only three persons, who represent to us the mystery of the most holy and most adorable Trinity; not that there is any comparison except with regard to our Lord, who is one of the Persons of the most Holy Trinity, for the others are creatures. But yet we may say that it is a Trinity on earth, which in a manner represents to us the most Holy Trinity: Mary, Jesus and Joseph; Joseph, Jesus and Mary; a Trinity marvelously estimable and worthy of being honored" (Conferences of St. Francis de Sales, Conference 19).

xxxvii See Ex 25:13; 25:28, 30:5; Deut 10:3.

xxxviii See Ex 25:10, 37: 1-9.

xxxix Ex 31:18, 25:51; Deut 10:2:5.

xl See Heb 9:4.

xli See Numb 17:8.

xlii See Ex 40:34.

xliii See Josh 5:13-6:27.

xliv See Josh 3.

xlv Lk 1:35: "And the angel answering, said to her: The Holy Ghost shall come upon thee, and the power of the Most High shall overshadow thee. And therefore, also the Holy which shall be born of thee shall be called the Son of God." The Greek word for overshadow, *episkiasei*, is the same word used in the Exodus account to describe God's Spirit overshadowing the Ark of the Covenant located in the tent of meeting.

+ JMJ +

xlvi  See Jn 1.
xlvii  See Jn 6.
xlviii  See Heb 4:14–16.
xlix  See Ps 2.
l  See Isa 11:1.
li  2 Sam 6:9: " And David was afraid of the Lord that day, saying: How shall the ark of the Lord come to me?"
lii  Lk 1:43: "And whence is this to me, that the mother of my Lord should come to me?"
liii  See Lk 1:28.
liv  See Isa 7:14.
lv  In Roman Catholic tradition, "Seat of Wisdom" or "Throne of Wisdom" (Latin *sedes sapientiae*) is one of many devotional titles for Mary, the Mother of God. It refers to her status as the vessel in which the Holy Child was born.
lvi  The Greek translation for the phrase "full of grace" is *kecharitomene*, which contains the Greek root word *charitoo* (which means "to give grace"). "The word [*kecharitomene*] is the past perfect tense, meaning that the action of giving grace had already occurred. It was not something that was about to happen to her but something that has already been accomplished. The word was also a title. The angel did not say, "Hail Mary, you are *kecharitomene*," but rather, "Hail, *kecharitomene*." Therefore, the word is not simply an action but an identity" (catholic.com/qa/full-of-grace-versus-highly-favored).
lvii  Lk 1:34: "And Mary said to the angel: How shall this be done, because I know not man?"
lviii  "Joseph's cooperation is constituted first and foremost by his consent to be the virginal husband of Mary. Again, to appeal to St. Thomas [Aquinas], we say that only by means of Joseph's matrimonial consent could that marriage have been brought into existence which was ordained to receive Christ. Only in the supposition of the marriage contract could Joseph agree with our Lady to live virginally within their union" (Filas, *Joseph and Jesus*).
lix  Reference to Psalm 1.
lx  See Mt 1:23.
lxi  See Isa 11:1.
lxii  See 2 Sam 6:7: "And the indignation of the Lord was enkindled against Oza, and he struck him for his rashness: and he died there before the ark of God."
lxiii  2 Sam 6:9.
lxiv  See footnotes 23 and 24.
lxv  Ibid.
lxvi  The name Jesus is derived from the Hebrew name Yeshua, which is based on the Semitic root y-š-ʕ (Hebrew: ישע), meaning «to deliver; to rescue.» Yeshua, and its longer form, Yehoshua, were both in common use by Jews during the Second Temple period» (https://en.wikipedia.org/wiki/Jesus).

lxvii 1 Sam 15:23.

lxviii CCC 400: "The harmony in which they had found themselves, thanks to original justice, is now destroyed: the control of the soul's spiritual faculties over the body is shattered; the union of man and woman becomes subject to tensions, their relations henceforth marked by lust and domination. Harmony with creation is broken: visible creation has become alien and hostile to man. Because of man, creation is now subject 'to its bondage to decay.' Finally, the consequence explicitly foretold for this disobedience will come true: man will 'return to the ground,' for out of it he was taken. *Death makes its entrance into human history.*"

lxix CCC 397: "Man, tempted by the devil, let his trust in his Creator die in his heart and, abusing his freedom, disobeyed God's command. This is what man's first sin consisted of. All subsequent sin would be disobedience toward God and lack of trust in his goodness."

lxx To obey (from the Latin *ob-audire*, to "hear or listen to») in faith is to submit freely to the word that has been heard, because its truth is guaranteed by God, who is Truth itself. Abraham is the model of such obedience offered us by Sacred Scripture. The Virgin Mary is its most perfect embodiment.

lxxi See Gen 3:12.

lxxii 1 Tim 2:6: "Who gave himself a redemption for all, a testimony in due times." And also: "Even as the Son of man is not come to be ministered unto, but to minister, and to give his life a redemption for many" (Mt 20:28).

lxxiii See Eph 5:22–33.

lxxiv For example: "My sister, my spouse, is a garden enclosed, a garden enclosed, a fountain sealed up" (Song 4:12).

lxxv St. Joseph and Mary were counted in the census as being among the human populace: "And Joseph also went up from Galilee, out of the city of Nazareth, into Judea, to the city of David, which is called Bethlehem: because he was of the house and family of David, to be enrolled with Mary his espoused wife, who was with child (Lk 2:4–5).

lxxvi 1 Jn 4:20: "If any man says, I love God, and hateth his brother; he is a liar. For he that loveth not his brother, whom he seeth, how can he love God, whom he seeth not?"

lxxvii Rom 13:1–2.

lxxviii Lk 16:10: "He that is faithful in that which is least, is faithful also in that which is greater: and he that is unjust in that which is little, is unjust also in that which is greater."

lxxix Quoting Origen, Pope St. John Paul II states: "Origen gives a good description of the theological significance, by no means marginal, of this historical fact: 'Since the first census of the whole world took place under Caesar Augustus, and among all the others Joseph too went to register together with Mary his wife, who was with child, and since Jesus was born before the census was completed: to the person who makes a careful examination it will appear that a kind of mystery is expressed in the fact that at the time when all people in the world presented themselves to be counted, Christ too should be counted. By being registered with everyone, he could sanctify everyone; inscribed with the whole world in the census, he offered to the world communion with himself, and after presenting himself he wrote all the people of the world in the book of the living, so that as many as believed in him could then be written in heaven with the saints of God, to whom

+ JMJ +

be glory and power for ever and ever, Amen'" (*Redemptoris Custos* 9).

lxxx    Micah 5:2: "AND THOU, BETHLEHEM Ephrata, art a little one among the thousands of Juda: out of thee shall he come forth unto me that is to be the ruler in Israel: and his going forth is from the beginning, from the days of eternity."

lxxxi    Rom 9:20: "O man, who art thou that repliest against God? Shall the thing formed say to him that formed it: Why hast thou made me thus?"

lxxxii    Jn 1:11: "He came unto his own, and his own received him not."

lxxxiii    See Col 3:1-3: "Therefore if you be risen with Christ, seek the things that are above, where Christ is sitting at the right hand of God. Mind the things that are above, not the things that are upon the earth. For you are dead: and your life is hid with Christ in God."

lxxxiv    See Rom 8:5.

lxxxv    Col 3:2.

lxxxvi    Lk 2:6.

lxxxvii See Heb 12.

lxxxviii    Heb 12:6.

lxxxix    See Lev 12; Ex 13:12–15.

xc    See Ex 12.

xci    See Jn 1:29.

xcii    Mt 25:14-30.

xciii    Lk 2:24.

xciv    Mt 5:3.

xcv    See endnote 53.

xcvi    See Psalm 110.

xcvii    2 Cor 9:7.

xcviii    Mk 12:41–44.

xcix    2 Cor 9:6.

c    Jn 15:13.

ci    Herod learned from the Magi the time of when the star appeared. This connected with the fact that he had the children of Bethlehem, two years and younger, slaughtered, indicates that approximately two years had passed. "Then Herod, privately calling the wise men, learned diligently of them the time of the star which appeared to them" (Mt 2:7).

cii    See Jn 4:20.

ciii    See Jn 9:3.

civ    1 Cor 3:16.

cv    See Mk 9:37; Mt 18:5.

cvi    See 1 Sam 2:12-36: Eli, the anointed priest of God, neglected to discipline his two sons, Hophni and Phinehas, who as temple priests, abused their rights, taking the spoils of the sacrifices and coercing women into illicit sexual relations. "Thus saith the Lord: Did I not plainly appear to thy father's house, when they were in Egypt in the house of Pharaoh? And I chose him out of all the tribes of Israel to be my priest, to go up to my altar, and burn incense to me, and to wear the ephod before me: and I gave to thy father's house of all the sacrifices of the children of Israel. Why have you kicked away my victims, and my gifts which I commanded to be offered in the temple: and **thou hast rather honored thy sons than me**, to eat the first fruits of every sacrifice of my people Israel?" (emphasis added).

cvii   Ps 127:1.

cviii  See James 1:17: "Every best gift, and every perfect gift, is from above, coming down from the Father of lights, with whom there is no change, nor shadow of alteration."

cix    (Ps 50:14 ASV):"Offer unto God the sacrifice of thanksgiving; And pay thy vows unto the Most High"

cx     Phil 4:11–12.

cxi    See 1 Thes 5:18.

cxii   1 Tim 6:17.

cxiii  Jn 8:44.

cxiv   Ibid.

cxv    Jn 10:10.

cxvi   Rev 12:4.

cxvii  Ps 8:2.

cxviii See CCC 221.

cxix   1 Pet 5:8.

cxx    See 1 Pet 5:10: "Whom resist ye, strong in faith: knowing that the same affliction befalls your brethren who are in the world."

cxxi   Mt 18:14.

cxxii  Isa 49:2.

cxxiii St. Thomas Aquinas, *Commentary on the Gospel of St. Matthew*, 234–36.

cxxiv  CCC 363.

cxxv   See CCC glossary, "Soul."

cxxvi  Mt 6:25.

cxxvii Lk 11:13.

cxxviii Mk 3:25: "And if a house be divided against itself, that house cannot stand."

cxxix  Analyzing the nature of marriage, both St. Augustine and St. Thomas always identify it with an "indivisible union of souls," a "union of hearts," with "consent." These elements are found in an exemplary manner in the marriage of Mary and Joseph. At the culmination of the history of salvation, when God reveals his love for humanity through the gift of the Word, it is precisely the marriage of Mary and Joseph that brings to realization in full "freedom" the "spousal gift of self" in receiving and expressing such a love. "In this great undertaking, which is the renewal of all things in Christ, marriage—it too purified and renewed—becomes a new reality, a sacrament of the New Covenant (GR 7, Pope John Paul II).

+ JMJ +

cxxx    See Ex 12.

cxxxi   See Jn 1:29.

cxxxii  See Gen 22:8.

cxxxiii See Jn 6:53.

cxxxiv "This is the bread which cometh down from heaven: that if any man eat of it, he may not die. I am the living bread which came down from heaven. If any man eat of this bread, he shall live for ever: and the bread that I will give is my flesh, for the life of the world" (Jn 6:50–51); "Then Jesus said to them: Amen, amen, I say unto you: except you eat the flesh of the Son of man and drink his blood, you shall not have life in you. He that eateth my flesh and drinketh my blood hath everlasting life: and I will raise him up in the last day. For my flesh is meat indeed: and my blood is drink indeed. He that eateth my flesh and drinketh my blood abideth in me: and I in him. As the living Father hath sent me and I live by the Father: so he that eateth me, the same also shall live by me. This is the bread that came down from heaven. Not as your fathers did eat manna and are dead. He that eateth this bread shall live for ever" (Jn 6:53–58).

cxxxv See Lk 12; Mt 24. In these passages, particularly Luke's version, our Lord succinctly outlines the major characteristics of the *Pater Familias*, ruler of the house: First, he has authority over his family as indicated by phrases "householder," "setteth over his family."

cxxxvi See Mk 14:22; Lk 22:19; 1 Cor 11:24.

cxxxvii See Mt 20:28.

cxxxviii   See Eph 5:23.

cxxxix  See endnote 132.

cxl     See Gen 22.

cxli    See Gen 22:6.

cxlii   Lk 2:44.

cxliii  See Jn 6:27.

cxliv   Mt 5:8.

cxlv    See Mt 18:14.

cxlvi   See Mal 4:6.

cxlvii  Lk 15:11–32.

cxlviii Lk 2:48/

cxlix   See Jn 3:30/

cl      See Rom 9:20/

cli     *Redemptoris Custos* 2, John Paul II.

clii    "Work was the daily expression of love in the life of the Family of Nazareth. The Gospel specifies the kind of work Joseph did in order to support his family: he was a carpenter. This simple word sums up Joseph's entire life. For Jesus, these were hidden years, the years to which Luke refers after recounting the episode that occurred in the Temple: "And he went down with them and came to Nazareth and was obedient to them" (Lk 2:51). This "submission" or obedience of Jesus in the house of Nazareth should be understood as a sharing in the work of Joseph. Having learned the work of his presumed father, he was known as "the carpenter's son." If the Family of Nazareth is an example and model for human families, in the order of salvation and holiness, so too, by analogy, is Jesus' work at the side of Joseph the carpenter. In our own day, the Church has emphasized this by instituting the liturgical memorial of St. Joseph the Worker on May 1. Human work, and especially manual labor, receive special prominence in the Gospel. Along with the humanity of the Son of God, work too has been taken up in the mystery of the Incarnation, and has also been redeemed in a special way. At the workbench where he plied his trade together with Jesus, Joseph brought human work closer to the mystery of the Redemption" (*Redemptoris Custos* 22, John Paul II)

cliii   See Eph 4:13.

cliv    See Gen 37–50.

clv     Gen 41:55.

clvi    Mt 24:45.

clvii   Pope Pius IX decreed officially that St. Joseph is patron of the Catholic Church and that his festival, occurring on March 19, is to be celebrated as a double of the first class. (Pius IX Decree, *Quemadmodum Deus*, December 8, 1870, which gives him the highest honor of any creature, except for the Immaculate Conception, Mary the Mother of God, *Theotokos*.) Therefore, by means of this position in the Church, he is ranked above all. As indicated by Pius IX's words, "That even as Blessed Joseph, though being the father of Christ, 'became so much superior to all creatures as he inherited a more excellent name than they,' so by a decree of the Congregation of Rites, the public *cultus* of dulia should in future be granted him in the universal Church and in the sacred liturgy, second to the Blessed Mother of God and before all the saints; That, St. Joseph, to whom the protection of the Holy Family was committed, should be made, next to the Blessed Virgin, the primary patron of the universal Church."

clviii  Col 3:1.

clix    Gen 41:55.